COOKBOOK

itsa Cookbook

Domini Kemp

Gill & Macmillan

Gill & Macmillan Ltd
Hume Avenue, Park West, Dublin 12
with associated companies throughout the world
www.gillmacmillan.ie

© Domini Kemp 2010
978 07171 4742 7

Photography by Joanne Murphy
Styling by Orla Neligan
Props supplied by Brown Thomas, Dublin, Cork, Galway, Limerick, tel. 01 605 6666;
www.brownthomas.com. Eden Home & Garden, 1–4 Temple Grove, Temple Road, Blackrock,
Co. Dublin; tel.: 01 764 2004; email: edenhomeandgarden@hotmail.com,
www.edenhomeandgarden.ie. Avoca Handweavers, H/O, Kilmacanogue, Bray, Co. Wicklow;
tel.: 01 286 7466; email: info@avoca.ie, www.avoca.ie. Meadows & Byrne, Dublin, Cork,
Galway, Clare, Tipperary; tel.: 01 280 5444/021 434 4100; email: info@meadowsandbyrne.com,
www.meadowsandbyrne.com
Index compiled by Cover to Cover
Design by Design Image, Dublin
Printed by GraphyCems, Spain

This book is typeset in 9 pt Humnst777 Lt BT on 16 pt.

The paper used in this book comes from the wood pulp of managed forests. For every tree
felled, at least one tree is planted, thereby renewing natural resources.

A CIP catalogue record for this book is available from the British Library.

5 4 3 2

For Lauren and Maeve,
our gorgeous girls

'...it may be said that while statesmen can carve nations, good cooks alone can consolidate them.'

Mrs Beeton's Cookery Year

Contents

Chapter 3 cont'd

CHAPTER FOUR: BIT ON THE SIDE

CHAPTER FIVE: SHOW-OFF

CHAPTER SIX: SWEET STUFF

Acknowledgments

My sincerest thanks to the dream team that worked so hard in helping to make the pictures look so gorgeous: Maisha Lenehan for being such a great cook and Orla Neligan for her Mary Poppins bags of props, plates and trinkets and her great sense of style. Joanne Murphy is not only a good friend, but also a wonderful photographer. Thanks ladies!

Thanks to Miss Lauren: a superb model and brilliant chocolate spoon cleaner.

Big thanks to all those who worked extra hard while I was finishing the book, namely Roark, Neil, Jerry, Caroline, Susan and Dermot. More big thanks to the restaurant managers and chefs as well as the itsa managers and all their crew. They do a brilliant job and we're lucky to have such great people working in the company.

I'm also extremely grateful to Patsey Murphy and Co. in the *Irish Times*, who are a pleasure to work with.

Thanks also to Fergal Tobin and all in Gill & Macmillan.

Ginormous thanks to Peaches, who should get the Oscar for Best Sister and Best Business Partner. She had to do the lion's share of work while I finished the book and was more than patient, understanding and supportive. Plus she makes the best Caesar salad dressing, so thanks for giving me your secret recipe. Cheers, Peachie!

And finally, the biggest thanks to Garvan, who is not only a great husband, but also a great father, reader, writer and minder of his gals. We're very lucky to have him.

Conversion charts

Oven

Degrees Celsius	Degrees Fahrenheit	Gas Mark	Description
140	275	1	very cool
150	300	2	cool
160	325	3	warm
180	350	4	moderate
190	375	5	fairly hot
200	400	6	fairly hot
220	425	7	hot
230	450	8	very hot
240	475	9	very hot

Weight

30 g	1 oz	425 g	15 oz
60 g	2 oz	450 g	1 lb
90 g	3 oz	500 g	18 oz
110 g	4 oz	570 g	1¼ lb
140 g	5 oz	680 g	1½ lb
170 g	6 oz	900 g	2 lb
200 g	7 oz	1 kg	2¼ lb
225 g	8 oz	1.1 kg	2½ lb
250 g	9 oz	1.4 kg	3 lb
280 g	10 oz	1.5 kg	3 lb 5 oz
310 g	11 oz	1.8 kg	4 lb
340 g	12 oz	2 kg	4½ lb
370 g	13 oz	2.2 kg	5 lb
400 g	14 oz		

Volume

5 ml	1 teaspoon	240 ml	8 fl oz
10 ml	1 dessertspoon	270 ml	9 fl oz
15 ml	1 tablespoon	300 ml	10 fl oz
30 ml	1 fl oz	325 ml	11 fl oz
60 ml	2 fl oz	350 ml	12 fl oz
90 ml	3 fl oz	400 ml	14 fl oz
120 ml	4 fl oz	450 ml	15 fl oz
150 ml	5 fl oz	475 ml	16 fl oz
175 ml	6 fl oz	1 litre	34 fl oz
200 ml	7 fl oz		

Introduction

My dear departed granny was always slim and elegant and I don't think I can ever remember a time when she said she was on a diet or dwelled too much about what she ate. She seemed to be the most perfect granny a kid could ask for and on special days, at 11.00 a.m. sharp, we shared a pack of cheese and onion crisps while I sipped a Cidona and she had a sherry.

Lunch was served at 1.00 p.m. and home-grown spuds cooked in the pressure cooker were always served. I'd be put in charge of making old-fashioned curls of butter, which were dropped onto the flouriest, most delicious spuds ever. Sometimes she'd make a 'chicken' stew, which was actually rabbit stew. Apparently I was going through a *Watership Down* love-in at the time and clearly couldn't handle the truth. I remember my grandfather would sit down at the table, breathe in and say, 'Ah, rabbit stew, my favourite.' As soon as he'd say it, he'd be on the receiving end of several kicks while being reminded yet again that it was 'chicken', not 'rabbit'. It wasn't long before I started to sense bunnycide.

The mountain of leftover spuds would be fried the next day with sautéed onions and loads of parsley in plenty of drippings left over from a roast. It was then served with scrambled eggs and a few rashers for our tea. It was damn fine food and a lesson in simple flavours and pleasures mixed in with family and fond memories.

When you think about it, cooking is universal and unique to humans and society as a whole. No other animal cooks, and although some food fascists try to survive on raw food alone, most of us cook. Today, our brains consume 20–25 per cent of the energy we stuff into ourselves, but until our Stone Age ancestors started cooking, it would have been hard to ingest enough calories to supply our brains as well as our bodies. This is why some scientists believe that cooking and humanity go hand in hand.

As anyone who owns a frying pan knows, cooking alters food considerably. But scrape it back scientifically and you'll find that it goes beyond making things taste good: cooking breaks down starches and denatures protein molecules so that their amino acid chains unfold and our digestive juices can break them down more effectively.

The downside for us *Homo sapiens* is that big food companies know only too well what our taste buds (and brains) crave. They spend small fortunes ensuring mouth feel is optimised so that we buy more of their soft, gooey cookies or smooth, creamy ice cream. Highly processed food full of empty calories is what our brains really love. Don't think for a moment that the giant food corporations don't know this!

I cook professionally and, together with my sister, run a number of restaurants, cafés and a catering company. But every day, I cook at home, where time, nutrition, satisfaction and taste are all key factors. I love to take a recipe, tear it apart, try to make it simpler and tastier and eliminate anything that isn't utterly critical. The aim of this book is to get you to cook rather than stare at a long list of ingredients and say, 'Nah, I think I'll order a take-away instead.'

If there's one thing I hope for, it's that some of these recipes become part of your repertoire – and subsequently, firm favourites.

Domini Kemp
August 2010

The Holy Grail of Basics

1

The following are some simple basics that, once mastered, will never let you down. Being able to cook a steak, make a good vinaigrette and roast a chicken are three things I would insist everyone should learn how to do before leaving home. Maybe baking a loaf of bread should also be on the list, along with making a good soup. What I'm trying to say is this: being able to cook a good, solid dinner is a grand skill to have. So read on.

Best ever vinaigrette

Makes approx. 800 ml

Now the type of dressing may vary, but the balance of oil to vinegar is key, which changes depending on sharpness or acidity and the variety of the vinegar itself. If I'm being very lazy but really decadent, I'll get a big bunch of baby spinach and drizzle some truffle oil directly into the bowl along with a squeeze of lemon juice, a handful of grated Parmesan, salt and pepper and give it a little toss. A really good aged sweet sherry vinegar can also produce a great result drizzled onto crisp Baby Gems with some fruity olive oil, salt and pepper. But my favourites are my sister's dressings.

Peaches has been making this salad dressing for as long as I can remember, and if we have supper together at home, it's usually a big salad that's served up, full of avocadoes, spring onions, tomatoes and anything else that's green and can be chucked in. She makes this in one big batch, storing it in an empty olive oil bottle, and keeps it in the fridge. It will solidify, so take it out of the fridge an hour before you need it, or else dunk the bottle into a bowl of hot water for a minute or two. It'll soon become liquid enough to shake and use.

500 ml olive oil
120 ml white wine vinegar
100 ml balsamic vinegar
4 cloves garlic, peeled and crushed
2 tbsp English mustard
2 tbsp ketchup
2 tbsp soy sauce
3 tbsp honey
2 tbsp Worcestershire sauce
salt and freshly ground black pepper

1. Whizz all the ingredients together. Season very well. Store in the fridge for 3 to 4 weeks.

A good dressing maketh the salad.

Also remember that searing gives flavour. That's all. Please don't be fooled into believing that by searing a steak you're 'sealing in' the juices.

Wrong. It's scientifically false.

Cooking a good steak

I was a vegetarian for about seven years when I was a young lass, but finally cracked one night after too much wine and the lure of a buttery bacon butty grilled to crispy, salty perfection. Once I'd broken my seven-year vegetable itch, I scratched it with a carnivorous vengeance and couldn't wait to chomp into a good steak.

A steak is one of my favourite things to eat at home as a treat, along with a Caesar salad. In fact, it would probably be a strong contender for my Death Row dinner. But so many people have a hard time getting restaurant-style steaks at home. Why? A lot of it is basic confusion about heat and the way meat actually cooks.

I think it's helpful to understand that when frying a piece of meat in a little olive oil on a hot, hot pan, the hiss and sizzle you hear is actually water escaping from the meat, hitting the pan and immediately vaporising. If you don't hear that constant and succulent sizzle, your pan isn't hot enough or you've overloaded your pan with too much meat.

The key to a great steak is getting a dark, tasty, caramelised crust to form (which can be speeded up by using a pinch of sugar as a seasoning) and to regularly flip your steak (at 20-second intervals) so that the heat diffuses, which in turn gives you a much juicier interior.

Also, never cook your steak straight from the fridge. It's much better to let it come to room temperature before cooking, but if I said keep it out for an hour, the food hygiene police would be giving out to me, so 15 to 30 minutes will do.

For those of you who like meat well done, try cooking your thick fillet steak in two thinner slices. A thinner piece of meat will cook much faster than a big thick one, as the heat can penetrate the middle much faster. Cooking a well-done steak is, well, a challenge. Most chefs will get cross if you ask for it well done, as they simply hate seeing a gorgeous 8 oz fillet shrivelling away to about 4 to 6 oz after it has been torched.

I marinate steaks in a few tablespoons of olive oil, a splash of soy sauce, a few sprigs of thyme, a few whole, peeled garlic cloves and lots of black pepper. Then I leave them for anything from an hour to overnight, turning them occasionally so that they get well coated in flavour. Bring them to room temperature and then heat up a teaspoon of oil in a stainless steel or iron pan or char-grill pan till very hot. Two to a pan is loads. Don't overload the pan or you'll end up stewing the steaks rather than frying them.

Sprinkle a pinch of caster or Demerara sugar onto the side you'll fry first, along with some salt and more pepper. Fry the steaks on one side and give them a minute or so, sprinkling the top side with sugar, salt and pepper. When they have released their fibres, they'll flip over easily. If they're sticking to the pan, leave them be. They will release themselves when they're ready. Once you have a good crust on each side, add a knob of butter and start flipping the steaks every 15 to 20 seconds and reduce the heat. At this stage, I sometimes add a splash of balsamic vinegar, Worcestershire sauce and a bit more soy sauce for a 'lazy wench' type of jus, which will deglaze the pan and contribute even more to a glossy, dark, restaurant-looking steak. But you don't have to do this, as they should have a really good dark crust on them anyway at this stage.

When you're happy with the colour, turn off the heat, move the pan to a colder part of the cooker and leave the steaks to rest there for another few minutes. The steaks should still seem tender and fleshy and this entire cooking process should only have taken about 8 minutes for medium-rare. Leave them to rest for 5 minutes before serving.

Remember to feel the meat. Feel the tightness in the meat gradually relax when you let it rest for a few minutes. Try to remember the fleshy feeling you get when meat is too rare. And drum it into your culinary senses how totally at odds this feeling of flabby torque is in comparison to the tough rigidity that takes over when you've cremated the thing.

Cooking a good steak requires practice and confidence.

Cooking a roast chicken

In recent years, the price of chicken has gone up rather significantly. Certain pedigree chickens are now around the €20 mark, which means they really ought to be treated like VIBs (very important birds). A roast chicken has become a bit of a luxury nowadays, so it should get a bit of loving regarding its prep for the oven.

For years, I was under the impression that trussed chickens would never cook properly. I blame my mother's generation for this particular bit of misinformation. Trussed chickens cook more evenly because the breast is slightly protected and less likely to dry out than one whose legs are splayed. I like to start off by rinsing a trussed bird in cold water, then roasting it breast side down on a bed of onions and carrots with garlic, thyme and lemon.

But the food hygiene police get very cagey about letting mere mortals rinse raw meat, as they worry that splashes of water coming from the chicken will contaminate things around your sink (cloths, cutlery, etc.) and potentially give you food poisoning. There are ways you can get around this, and one is a little organisation! Have the roasting tin ready and close to your sink. Run the tap very gently and have some washing-up liquid poured out onto a little saucer. Take your bird, rinse gently (avoiding big splashes) and place in the roasting tin immediately. You can wash your hands with the tap still running and when you feel they are clean, turn up the hot tap and wash well. Spray down the sink area with a disinfectant and you should be fine. What you're trying to avoid is washing your bird, having lots of water splash all over the place, handling the taps or oven door or fridge door with contaminated hands and then leaving a dirty sink that you might wash fruit or veg in later.

Make a bed of peeled and roughly chopped carrots, baby spuds, onions, loads of lemons and garlic and a handful of thyme. Put the chicken on top, breast side down, and douse the chicken with a glass of white wine before sprinkling with sea salt and black pepper. I usually roast on a high heat (190°C), until the legs are pretty much cooked through. Then I turn the chicken over, splash the bird with some more wine and sometimes drizzle it with a tiny bit of honey, a smear of Dijon mustard or a splash of Worcestershire sauce, and put it back in the oven for another blast, giving the skin a chance to crisp up. Despite knowing how, I don't think I've ever bothered to make chicken stock at home from the leftover bones, which I really *should* be doing. I compensate instead by scraping every bit of meat off the carcass, which does make a good school lunch or two.

See overleaf for recipe.

Roast chicken

2 heads garlic, unpeeled
2 carrots, peeled and roughly chopped
2 onions, roughly chopped (unpeeled)
1 medium chicken, approx. 1.5 kg
2 lemons, cut in half
2 glasses white wine
a few sprigs of thyme
salt and freshly ground black pepper
1 tbsp honey (optional)

1. Preheat the oven to 190°C. Put the garlic, carrots and onions in the middle of a roasting tray. I sometimes slice one head in half horizontally and leave the cloves of the other head loose but unpeeled. Give the chicken a good rinse in cold water (see p. 7), then place breast side down on top of the veg – don't worry if it's wet.

2. Squeeze the lemons over the chicken, then stuff the lemon halves into the cavity. Pour the wine over next and then season generously with thyme, salt and pepper. Cover in tin foil and roast for about 35 minutes.

3. Remove the foil, flip the bird over and squeeze some honey on top. Season again and cook for another 15 to 20 minutes. At this stage, take it out and leave for a few minutes. Give the legs a wiggle: they should move about freely. If you aren't sure, slice between the leg and the breast and check the colour. It shouldn't be too pink and the juices should definitely be clear.

4. Carve up after resting for 10 minutes and serve with the roasted garlic, carrots and onions.

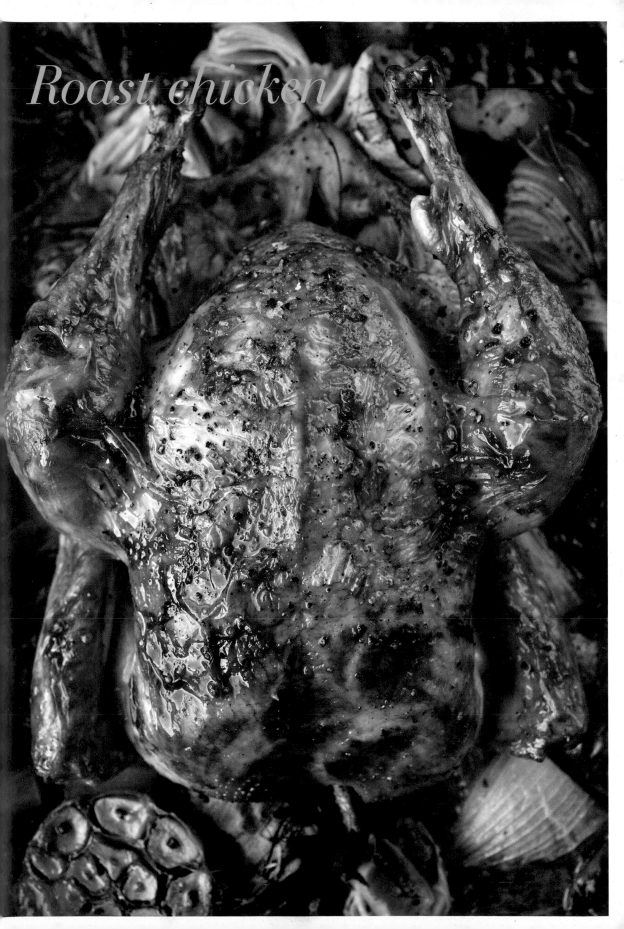

Roast chicken

Brekkie, Brunch and Elevenses

What do we normally eat for brekkie? Well, certainly nothing in this chapter, if the truth be told. For me, it might be some muesli with milk and a banana or half a pumpernickel bagel with peanut butter, a cup of tea and some juice. If I can get two pieces of fruit into everyone in the house in the morning, then I'm pretty happy, as we're then nearly halfway to getting our five a day. If time is short, then a handful of nuts and dried fruit as well as a banana do the trick. Home-made smoothies are also great: I usually use frozen fruit for them, as fresh berries are too pricey year round and probably chalk up too many air miles. Into the blender goes a big blob of plain yoghurt, some frozen fruit and a splash of apple juice. If I can bear it, a carrot and a beetroot get chucked in and off we gulp.

But the dishes in this chapter are for when breakfast is a bit of an occasion and when you've got a few spare hours in the morning or you want to make something as a treat on a rainy afternoon. There's something very appealing about cooking brunch for friends or enjoying a piece of cake and a cup of tea in the afternoon – you can entertain on the cheap and get rid of people before dark. That may sound a bit cruel, but peppy and cheap are always good fun. Naturally there won't be any red wine teeth or the endless stream of babble that happens at dinner parties, but that can easily be recreated with a few Bloody Marys and Bellinis!

Spinach, sorrel and Gruyère tart

Serves 4

Cheese is my big downfall. I could happily gorge on good cheese and bread forever, with a few bits of fruit and quince jelly thrown in. I especially love a good Gruyère reserve cheese that has those crystals in it that also form in Parmesan cheese during the ageing process, when moisture levels drop and crystals form as a result. It imparts an unctuous, nutty flavour and when I taste it, I'm reminded what a perfect food cheese really is. Although I hate to use such a fine cheese in a tart (I'd rather eat it on its own), it's well worth it, as you should make these tarts as a special treat for someone you're very fond of. Needless to say, use whatever cheese you love and use whatever combo of spinach and/or sorrel you want.

Spinach, sorrel and Gruyère tart

270 g filo pastry

300 g spinach, either big leaf or baby

100 g sorrel

3 eggs

200 ml cream

a pinch of ground nutmeg (optional)

a pinch of cayenne pepper

250 g grated Gruyère

salt and freshly ground black pepper

50 g melted butter

100 g pine nuts, lightly toasted

green salad, to serve

You will also need 4 x 12 cm tart tins.

1. Take the filo pastry out to defrost. Keep it covered with a damp tea towel and unravel it as it thaws. Don't worry too much if it breaks up a bit, but keep it covered.
2. Preheat the oven to 200°C.
3. Remove any stalky bits if you're using big leaf spinach (this isn't necessary if you're using the baby leaf kind). Blanch the sorrel and spinach together in boiling water for a few seconds, then drain and squeeze the living daylights out of it using a clean tea towel. If you're using baby spinach, just wilt it with a knob of butter in a frying pan instead, but do dry it out just as well. Roughly chop up the greens and set aside.
4. Beat the eggs, then add the cream, nutmeg and cayenne. Mix well, then add the cheese and season.
5. Brush the tart tins with a little melted butter and place on a baking tray. Line the tins with individual squares of filo pastry that you've cut so that the sheets slightly hang over the edges. Do about five layers of filo in each tin, brushing the sheets generously and regularly with melted butter. You may have to patch any gaps.
6. Spoon equal amounts of the spinach, sorrel and cheese mixture into each tin, making sure to distribute it evenly. Carefully pour the egg mixture on top and scatter the pine nuts over. Bake for 12 to 15 minutes, until the topping is golden brown. Allow to cool for about 30 minutes, then carefully remove from the tins. Serve with a crisp green salad.

Apricot and orange muffins

Makes 12 muffins

I love these muffins, and even though it might seem a bit decadent to put fresh OJ into some muffin batter, it gives them a great flavour.

250 g dried apricots
juice and zest of 2 oranges
375 g plain flour
4 tsp baking powder
125 g butter, softened
150 g caster sugar
2 large eggs
250 ml plain yoghurt
2 tbsp honey

1. Preheat the oven to 200°C. Grease a muffin tin and put it in the freezer while you prep the muffin mix.
2. Chop the apricots as finely as you can and soak in the orange juice along with the zest for 30 minutes.
3. Sift the flour and baking powder together and set aside. Beat the softened butter and sugar until light and fluffy, then slowly whisk in the eggs and yoghurt. Ignore the curdling or chuck in a spoon of flour to make it go away. Add the honey, apricots and juice and zest. Mix well, then fold in the flour and baking powder mixture until just combined (don't overmix).
4. Spoon the batter into the muffin tray. Fill a small saucepan or roasting tray with 2 cups of water and put it on the same shelf beside the muffin tray, as the steam helps keep them extra moist. Bake for 25 minutes.

Tip: When they're cooked and you've taken them out of the oven, place the muffin tray on a damp cloth, as the muffins should then pop out more easily onto a wire rack.

P.S. I've forgotten to put water in the oven with the muffins, and they're still lovely and moist.

Muffins

Soda bread

Grandmother McGrath's soda bread

Makes 1 loaf

I managed to extract this recipe from the Cliff House Hotel in Waterford, which serves this delicious bread with a crab salad on top. I've adapted it from the original just a little bit, as I found the mixture a bit too dry when mixing it. Then again, it means you have to bake it for longer. Apologies, Granny McGrath!

350 g coarse ground whole-wheat flour
150 g cream flour
100 g wheat germ
100 g porridge oats
100 g bran
100 g soft brown sugar
1 tbsp bicarbonate of soda
a pinch of salt
2 large eggs
900 ml buttermilk
a good squeeze of honey

You will also need 1 big loaf tin, approx. 31 cm x 11 cm x 7 cm.

1. Preheat the oven to 170°C. Grease the loaf tin with butter.
2. Put all the dry ingredients into a large mixing bowl.
3. Whisk the eggs and mix with the buttermilk and honey, then add it to the dry ingredients. Mix really well, making sure all the flour gets well mixed with the wet ingredients. Pour the bread mix into the greased loaf tin.
4. Place the tin on a baking sheet and bake for at least 80 minutes. Remove from the oven and allow to cool slightly before slicing.

Granola goodness

Makes approx. 12 bars

I know it's naive to imagine you could ever get something decent to eat in a petrol station, which is why I've become one of those annoying people who stashes packs of dried fruit, water, oatcakes and fresh fruit in my bag for road trips. These granola bars are great as you can freeze them, wrapped individually, for just such occasions.

Don't worry if you have to substitute one type of nut for another. You can also try changing the dried fruit. I don't think it'll make much difference. Do make sure you leave them in the tin to cool and possibly chill them before slicing. If you don't bake them for long enough or leave them to set till hard they tend to crumble, but they still taste great!

45 g pecans
100 g figs, finely chopped
45 g dried apricots, finely chopped
45 g dried sour cherries (or cranberries)
200 g oats
45 g pumpkin seeds
30 g sesame seeds
30 g ground almonds
a good pinch of cinnamon
100 ml olive oil
4 tbsp honey
75 g Demerara sugar

1. Preheat the oven to 150°C.
2. Lightly toast the pecans for 5 to 10 minutes on a baking tray in the oven. Soak the figs, apricots and cherries in a small amount of just-boiled water for 5 minutes, then drain. Roughly chop the pecans, then mix with the oats, seeds, almonds, cinnamon and the chopped fruit.
3. Heat the olive oil, honey and sugar in a small saucepan till the sugar dissolves, then mix well with the fruit and nuts.

Granola goodness

4. Line a tin with parchment paper (mine is a rectangular tin that measures 20 cm in one direction). Using a wet spatula, pack the granola mix into the tin and smooth the top. Keep dipping the spatula into some water, as this helps smooth it down without sticking. Bake for 25 minutes, or until it's starting to turn golden brown.

5. Allow to cool fully in the tin, then remove from the tin and cut into bars. Wrap well in cling film and freeze, or keep in the fridge.

St Tola goat's cheese and thyme soufflé

Serves 4 to 6

This recipe was given to me by the makers of St Tola cheese, although I believe it originated in Alice Waters's restaurant, Chez Panisse, in California. If you aren't lucky enough to get St Tola cheese, use any soft goat's cheese.

1 small onion, halved
3 cloves
300 ml milk
300 ml cream
1 bay leaf
½ tsp black peppercorns
75 g butter
40 g plain flour

5 large eggs, separated
175 g soft St Tola goat's cheese
1 tbsp thyme leaves, plus a few extra
    to garnish
¼ tsp cayenne pepper
freshly ground black pepper
green salad, to serve

1. Preheat the oven to 200°C. Lightly butter a shallow oval ovenproof dish that measures 30 cm x 18 cm and about 5 cm deep. (You can also do this in individual ramekins.)
2. Stud the onion halves with the cloves and put them into a saucepan along with the milk, cream, bay leaf and peppercorns. Bring to the boil, then remove from the heat and set aside for 20 minutes to infuse. Strain the milk and cream through a sieve and discard the onion, bay leaf and peppercorns.
3. Melt the butter in a saucepan, then add the flour and cook over a medium heat for 1 minute to cook out the flour. Gradually whisk in the flavoured milk and cream. Whisk until smooth and lump free, then remove from the heat and cool slightly before beating in the egg yolks, cheese, thyme and cayenne pepper. Season with loads of black pepper.
4. Whisk the egg whites until they form soft peaks and gently fold them into the mixture.
5. Pour the soufflé mixture into the buttered dish and bake for 30 minutes, until the top is puffed up and golden but the centre is still soft and creamy. Garnish with a few thyme leaves. Serve with a green salad.

Soufflé

Super-light carrot cake

Serves 8

This has to be my favourite carrot cake recipe. I think the key to its success is the amount of raw carrots in it. It's adapted from Tessa Kiros's wonderful cookbook, *Falling Cloudberries*.

for the cake:
4 eggs
250 g caster sugar
185 ml sunflower oil
300 g flour
2 tsp baking powder
1 tsp bicarbonate of soda
2 tsp cinnamon
a pinch of salt
400 g grated carrots

for the icing:
200 g cream cheese, softened
200 g icing sugar
175 g butter, softened
zest of 1 lemon

You will also need a 24 cm springform tin.

1. Preheat the oven to 180°C. Grease the springform tin and line the bottom with parchment paper.
2. Beat the eggs and the caster sugar with an electric beater till pale, thick and creamy, about 5 to 10 minutes. Add the sunflower oil and beat until combined.
3. Sieve all the dry ingredients together, then fold into the egg and sugar mixture. Stir in the carrots, mixing well to combine.
4. Pour the batter into the prepared tin and bake for 1 hour 15 minutes, or until a skewer comes out clean.
5. Meanwhile, to make the icing, mix all the ingredients together by hand, rather than a beater. Make sure the butter is soft, otherwise it won't combine well with the cream cheese and will stay lumpy. This makes enough icing to do the outside of the cake only. If you want to slice the cake in half horizontally and ice the middle as well, make 1.5 times the recipe for the icing.

Kitchen sink frittata

Serves 3 to 4 as a main course for supper if served with some salad, or serves 6 for brunch

When asked what my favourite ingredient is, I'd probably have to say an egg. It may be a dull, lifeless shell on the outside, but inside, it's full of nutrients and goodness and is the ultimate fast food, the bedrock of all cakes, ice creams and savoury tarts and is equally essential for rich emulsions.

To make a good frittata, you need a heavy-based saucepan (22–25 cm) with an ovenproof handle. Feel free to chuck most things into this: leeks, courgettes, broccoli or anything green, for that matter, or substitute the goat's cheese with halloumi, cheddar or brie.

a tiny splash of olive oil
2 red onions, sliced
1 bunch asparagus
2 handfuls baby spinach – about 100 g spinach in total
10 cherry tomatoes, halved
salt and freshly ground black pepper
6 eggs
200 ml milk
250 g goat's cheese

1. Preheat the oven to 180°C.
2. Heat the splash of olive oil and fry the onions over a high heat for a few minutes, until they're just starting to colour.
3. Meanwhile, trim the woody ends off the asparagus and cut into bite-sized pieces. Place the asparagus in a colander and pour a kettle of boiling water over them to just cook them a little – what I call lazy wench blanching. Drain, then add to the pan.
4. Add the spinach and tomatoes and stir until the spinach just wilts. Season well, then take off the heat.
5. Beat the eggs and milk together. Pour the egg mixture over the vegetables in the pan and scatter the cheese on top.
6. Bake for about 20 minutes, until just set. Allow to cool for at least 5 minutes, then serve.

P.S. Be conscious of the salt factor. Goat's cheese or halloumi can be quite salty, and if you add ham or rashers, then you need to watch it with the seasoning.

'Anything you fancy' savoury tarts

Makes 4 tarts

For a light supper, serve one tart per person and feel free to stick whatever you like on it – within reason, of course. Try some pesto, vary the cheeses or even sauté some mushrooms and dot with Taleggio and rosemary. Most cheese combinations will go perfectly well with a nice green salad and glass of something white and crisp.

4 ready-rolled puff pastry discs
1 tbsp olive oil
a knob of butter
2 onions, thinly sliced
a sprinkle of caster sugar (optional)
salt and freshly ground black pepper
400 g Gubbeen cheese, sliced
1 x 250 g punnet of cherry tomatoes (allow about 5 per tart)
a few sprigs of thyme

1.   Preheat the oven to 200°C. Line a baking tray with parchment paper. Put the pastry discs onto the tray and let them thaw while you cook the onions.
2.   Heat the olive oil in a frying pan. Add the butter and sauté the onions for about 10 minutes over a very gentle heat, until brown and caramelised. You can speed this up by adding a good pinch of sugar. Season and allow to cool slightly before spooning the caramelised onions onto the pastry, leaving a 1 cm rim around the edge free of all toppings.
3.   Add slices of cheese, the halved cherry tomatoes, thyme and plenty of black pepper. Drizzle with a bit of olive oil, then either leave in the fridge for a few hours until ready to bake, or cook for about 20 minutes, until golden brown.

Anything you fancy

Apple, pear and muesli crumble

Serves 6 to 8

A healthy alternative to a tasty crumble, this is lovely with a big blob of yoghurt. Use any kind of good eating apples, such as Pink Lady, Granny Smith, Cox or Jazz.

200 ml apple juice
4 apples
4 pears
1–2 tsp cinnamon (optional)
300 g muesli
50 ml olive oil
a few tablespoons of honey
yoghurt, to serve

1. Preheat the oven to 200°C.
2. Pour the apple juice into a large bowl. Peel and dice the fruit and add it to the bowl with the apple juice. Sprinkle with cinnamon and mix well. Transfer the fruit into a Pyrex dish or other ovenproof dish.
3. Mix the muesli with the olive oil and sprinkle it on top of the fruit. Drizzle the honey on top of the muesli and bake for about 30 to 40 minutes, until the topping is starting to brown. Serve warm or cold with yoghurt.

27

Sweet corn fritters with tomato salsa

Sweet corn fritters with tomato salsa

Serves 6 to 8 as part of brunch

Although sweet corn is not my favourite ingredient, these make a nice change to serve at brunch. They would also be delicious served with some guacamole, as they're quite light and so can do with being paired up with richer ingredients like eggs and bacon. The salsa is good to serve with the fritters for colour and zing. The fritters can be prepped a few hours ahead of time or even the day before and reheated on a baking tray in a moderate oven (160°C).

for the sweet corn fritters:
250 g flour
1 tbsp sugar
1 tsp baking powder
½ tsp smoked paprika (optional)
¼ tsp salt
2 eggs, beaten
125 ml milk
1 x 320 g tin sweet corn, drained
1 bunch spring onions, chopped
small bunch coriander, roughly
   chopped
sunflower oil, for pan frying

for the tomato salsa:
4 tomatoes, finely diced
1 small red onion, very finely diced
½ small red chilli, deseeded and
   chopped
1 tsp sweet chilli sauce
½ tsp caster sugar
juice of 2 limes
small bunch coriander, finely chopped
salt and freshly ground black pepper

1. To make the fritters, dump everything into a bowl except for the sunflower oil and mix well. It should be the consistency of thick, gooey porridge.
2. Heat the sunflower oil in a frying pan. Plop spoonfuls of the corn mixture into the hot oil. Fry the fritters for 1 or 2 minutes on each side. Pat them down slightly while they're cooking in the pan, as they will cook better if a bit thinner.
3. To make the salsa, mix all the ingredients together and leave to marinate for 30 minutes at room temperature before serving.
4. Serve the fritters with the tomato salsa.

Peanut butter and chocolate chip cookies

Makes about 20 cookies

150 g unsalted peanuts
100 g butter
120 ml olive oil
6 tbsp smooth peanut butter
110 g soft brown sugar
1 egg
2 tsp vanilla extract
225 g caster sugar
275 g flour
1 tsp bicarbonate of soda
a pinch of salt
100 g dark chocolate chips

1. Preheat the oven to 180°C.
2. Toast the peanuts for a few minutes in the oven on a baking tray, being careful they don't burn. Lightly chop and set aside.
3. Lightly butter 2 baking trays. Beat the butter, olive oil, peanut butter and brown sugar for a couple of minutes, until well blended. Add the egg, vanilla and caster sugar and keep beating. Don't worry if it looks like it's going to curdle – add a spoon of flour and it'll be grand. Fold in the flour, bicarbonate of soda and salt, then fold in the peanuts and the chocolate chips.
4. Using a tablespoon, drop spoonfuls of the cookie dough onto the baking sheet. Dip the spoon in cold water if the mixture starts to stick too much, or dip your fingers in water to help place the blobs of cookie dough well spaced apart on the baking trays. Bake for 20 minutes, until golden brown. Cool on a wire rack until crisp.

Apple and pecan mini muffins

Makes 24 small muffins

When I see the word 'muffin', I get cranky because more often than not, commercial muffins are a stodgy mass of cheapo vegetable oils and fake flavourings. Next time you buy a muffin, put it in a paper bag and see how much cheap grease is absorbed by the bag. In stark contrast, these muffins are just gorgeous. The apples, a hint of crème fraîche, cinnamon and pecans yield a light but rich recipe, adapted from Diana Henry's beautiful cookbook, *Roast Figs, Sugar Snow*.

125 g pecans, roughly chopped
250 g soft brown sugar
a good pinch of cinnamon
400 g plain flour
2 tsp baking powder
100 g butter, melted
2 big cooking apples, peeled, cored and diced
200 ml crème fraîche
1 egg, beaten
a splash of milk

1. Preheat the oven to 180°C.
2. Mix the pecans, sugar and cinnamon together and set aside. If you're a good cook, sieve the flour into a large bowl. If you're slovenly, don't bother. Add the baking powder, butter, apples, crème fraîche, egg, milk and half the nutty sugar mix. Mix until combined well, but don't mix the heck out of it.
3. Spoon the batter into a non-stick muffin tray or into muffin cases. The mixture is quite dry, so it's hard to pack the mix into the cases, which is why they make perfect mini-muffins. Sprinkle the remainder of the nutty sugar mix on top of each muffin and bake for about 25 to 30 minutes, until a knife comes out clean.

Rhubarb and cinnamon squares

Makes about 12 squares

Afternoon tea in a swanky hotel is a big treat, with tiered trays, cake stands and clotted cream overflowing onto a table with a chintz backdrop. But if truth be told, a piece of this rhubarb and cinnamon cake and a nice cuppa does me nicely.

I've adapted this from a BBC *Good Food* recipe. Sometimes I think I should have added more sugar to the rhubarb mixture, but when you taste all the flavours together, it really works.

500 g rhubarb
100 g butter, softened
100 g golden caster sugar
1 large egg
250 g dark muscavado sugar
100 g mixed nuts, roughly chopped
1 tsp cinnamon
approx. 300 ml sour cream
225 g cream flour
1 tsp bicarbonate of soda
a pinch of salt

1. Preheat the oven to 180°C. Butter a rectangular baking tin (approx. 33 cm x 23 cm), then line with parchment paper.
2. Remove the end bits from the rhubarb and cut the rest into bite-size pieces – 500 g of rhubarb should leave you with 300 g of perfectly chopped rhubarb.
3. Beat the soft butter with the caster sugar until fluffy, then beat in the egg. Gently beat in the muscavado sugar, nuts, cinnamon and sour cream. Fold in the dry ingredients and the rhubarb.
4. Pour into the tin and bake for 35 to 40 minutes, or until a skewer comes out clean. Leave to cool, then cut into squares. This lasts for 4 to 5 days in the fridge.

Gingerbread

Makes 1 loaf

This is a slightly modified version of a Marcus Wareing recipe. The best bit is the crunchy topping that comes courtesy of the Demerara sugar sprinkled on top. And yes, that isn't a typo – you really do need 2 tablespoons of ground ginger for this recipe.

200 g golden syrup
150 g butter, softened
100 g caster sugar
1 egg
100 ml milk
2 tbsp ground ginger
2 tsp ground cinnamon
250 g cream flour
1 tsp bicarbonate of soda
50 g Demerara sugar

1. Preheat the oven to 160°C. Grease a loaf tin and line the bottom with parchment paper.
2. Heat the golden syrup till just runny. Add the butter and sugar and heat gently, until the butter melts and the sugar dissolves. Take off the heat.
3. Beat together the egg, milk and spices and whisk into the golden syrup mixture. Pour in the flour and bicarbonate of soda and beat until fully mixed. Pour the batter into the tin and sprinkle with the Demerara sugar.
4. Bake for 20 minutes, then cover with tin foil that's been greased with butter. Bake for another 40 minutes, until a skewer inserted into the gingerbread is kind of clean. Rest in the tin for a couple of hours, then remove and slice. This keeps well in an airtight container for a few days, no problem.

No-fuss Dinners

What do we want to eat midweek? Countless cookbooks have been dedicated to solving this very conundrum. Food companies have made a mint out of this dilemma by selling an endless supply of ready-made meals. And why? Maybe it's down to our lack of time or energy when it comes to feeding ourselves or our families. Maybe it's because when we're wrecked from work, we have little or no appetite for more work in the kitchen and the lure of the take-away or home delivery throbs in our heads and gnaws at our stomachs. Sometimes we want to eat something that's comforting and warming. Sometimes we just need to be fed.

Midweek dinners are a time to feed and also a time to be well fed, but when you don't necessarily want to consume loads of heavy grub or too many useless calories. You want to feel satisfied and yet want to eat something balanced and nutritious. In our house, we try not to eat meat every night, so lots of what we eat is actually vegetarian. As a society, we're being told that we eat far too much meat, mainly because it has become so much cheaper, and as countries and societies get richer, demand for meat grows in leaps and bounds.

I try to have one meat-based dish during the week and the rest of the time is spent eating vegetarian dishes with pulses or simple pasta dishes, which I like to make using whole-wheat pasta. If I can get two meals out of one dish, so much the better, which is why dishes like the vegetable lentil soup, barley stew or the duck dal are so handy. Some, though not all, of the meat-based recipes take into account the fact that you don't necessarily have hours to marinate or slowly simmer before dinner, so they produce results with less time. But the ones that do require time don't take much effort to prep in order to get it in the oven.

All in all, these no-fuss dinners form the bedrock of what I cook at home for dinner.

Lazy green Thai-ish curry

Serves 8

Get your blender or food processor out for this one. If you forget to buy lemongrass, for example, don't worry. Just add in more of the other stuff, like garlic and ginger. Double the recipe and freeze half of it (once it's cooled down to room temperature and then cooled in the fridge for an hour or so) in a plastic container. Then, when you want your own snazzy ready-made dinner, defrost and heat in a saucepan till piping hot. Serve with any kind of rice you fancy. I like jasmine.

for the green curry base:
6 cloves garlic, peeled
4 stalks lemongrass, roughly chopped
4 green chillies, seeds removed
2 onions, roughly chopped
2 giant thumbs' worth of ginger, peeled (add more if you like it!)
2 big bunches coriander, rinsed lightly and the stalks left on
juice and zest of 4 limes
4 tbsp fish sauce
2 tbsp sweet chilli sauce

for the curry:
6 to 8 skinless chicken breasts
2 onions, peeled
500 g button mushrooms (2 big handfuls)
4 aubergines
2 to 3 tbsp sunflower oil
500 ml water
2 x 400 g tins coconut milk (low-fat is grand)
2 bunches spring onions, finely chopped
2 big handfuls basil and coriander, roughly torn or chopped
rice, to serve

1. To make the green curry base, whizz all the ingredients together until it resembles green sludge. If your food processor jams, add a little water to help it along.

2. Chop the chicken into bite-sized pieces and chuck into a large bowl. Pour the green curry base on top. Mix well so the chicken is well coated and leave for anything between 10 minutes and overnight, whatever you can manage.

3. Chop the vegetables into bite-sized pieces. Heat the oil in a large saucepan and cook the onions and mushrooms over a high heat until starting to colour. Add the aubergines and watch them suck up all the juice. Season with a little salt or a splash of soy sauce. Don't worry if the aubergines start to burn in patches.

4. Add the water, then the marinated chicken. Mix well and add the coconut milk. Bring up to a gentle boil, then leave to simmer gently for about 30 to 40 minutes, stirring occasionally. Taste and serve with chopped spring onions, chopped herbs and rice.

Irish rarebit

Serves 4

Don't forget: Worcestershire sauce contains anchovy essence, so beware if you're feeding a veggie.

400 g grated cheddar
2 egg yolks
2 tbsp Worcestershire sauce
2 tbsp wholegrain mustard
8 slices brown bread
2 tomatoes, thinly sliced
freshly ground black pepper

1. Preheat the grill to medium.
2. Mix the cheddar, egg yolks, Worcestershire sauce and mustard together. Spoon on top of the brown bread, top with a slice or two of tomato and some black pepper. Grill until golden brown, which will happen quite quickly because of the egg.

Vegetable lentil soup

Serves 8

This soup is possibly the bedrock of our company. We've made thousands and thousands of batches of this soup over the last 10 years and it has a cult following, mainly because it's low fat, gluten free and vegan. I regularly make this at home, especially if anyone's got a cold or just feeling a bit low. For those of you interested in the small print, this recipe makes approx. 2.5 litres. A generous single portion of soup is around 250 ml. A small carrot weighs about 100 g and a smallish onion about 150 g.

1 tbsp sunflower or olive oil
1.5 kg carrots, sliced
1 kg white onions, diced
1 head celery, chopped
75 g Swiss Marigold Vegan bouillon
2 tbsp sweet chilli sauce
600 g red lentils
salt and freshly ground black pepper

Additional flavours to chuck in at the beginning include a large knob of ginger, peeled and thinly sliced, 6 cloves garlic, peeled and crushed, and a splash of soy sauce.

1. Heat the oil in a large pot. Add the carrots, onions and celery and sweat for 5 minutes. Add the flavourings, if using, the stock and sweet chilli sauce and mix well. Cook for another minute, then add enough water to cover – about 2 to 3 litres.
2. Rinse the lentils in a sieve under running water, then add them to the pot. Cover with a lid and cook for about 30 minutes at a gentle simmering boil, until the lentils are soft and the veg is tender. Season if necessary.

Vegetable lentil soup

Balsamic roast chicken with rocket, roast tomatoes and Parmesan

Serves 4

Quick, easy and reliable.

4 chicken breasts or supremes, skin on or off
a few tablespoons of olive oil
a few tablespoons of balsamic vinegar
a few cloves garlic, peeled
fresh thyme or rosemary if you have it
salt and freshly ground black pepper
1 x 250 g punnet of cherry tomatoes, halved
4 handfuls rocket
a few chunky shavings of Parmesan or Pecorino, to serve

1. Preheat the oven to 180°C.
2. Plop the chicken into a roasting tray (wash your hands after!) and pour over the olive oil and balsamic vinegar. Add in some garlic and herbs and season well. Add in the cherry tomatoes or leave them out if you don't like them.
3. Cover the roasting tray with a baking tray to form a lid (this just stops it from drying out too much, but foil will do) and cook for 10 minutes. Remove the lid/foil, turn the chicken pieces over and baste with the cooking juices. Give it another blast for another 5 to 10 minutes, until the chicken is fully cooked through. If you aren't sure or if your chicken breasts are ginormous, then just slice one in half lengthways and give it a few more minutes if it looks a little pink.
4. Arrange the rocket on 4 plates. Top with the chicken and some tomatoes and loads of cooking juices (which is like a warm and simple vinaigrette). Top with some Parmesan shavings and serve.

nigiano

Coriander chicken

Coriander chicken

Serves 4

I make this all the time as it's relatively healthy and quick, plus kids and husbands are happy to eat it. I often don't have fresh herbs to hand, so this can be made with a blob of yoghurt, some dried herbs, a squeeze of lemon juice and seasoning. This is also delicious served cold in sandwiches the next day.

200 g Greek yoghurt (half a big tub)
juice of 2 limes or lemons
1 tsp coriander seeds, lightly crushed
1 tsp sea salt
freshly ground black pepper
1 big bunch coriander (approx. 25 g), roughly chopped
4 skinless chicken breasts, cut into strips
olive oil
chickpea, feta and coriander salad (p. 46), to serve

1. Mix the yoghurt with the lime juice, coriander seeds, and salt and pepper. The easiest way to crush the seeds (if you don't have a pestle and mortar) is to put them in a cup and squish them with one end of a rolling pin. Mix the chopped coriander in with the yoghurt. Add the chicken and mix well. If you can marinate this for anything from 1 hour to overnight, it'll be much better.

2. Turn the grill up to high and spread the chicken onto a baking tray or roasting tin. Drizzle with some olive oil and grill for 7 to 10 minutes, turning the chicken occasionally as the yoghurt chars quite easily. When it's cooked through, serve hot or warm with the chickpea, feta and coriander salad on p. 46.

Chickpea, feta and coriander salad

Serves 4 to 6 as a side dish or 2 to 3 as a main course

approx. 200 ml olive oil
2 red onions, very finely sliced
5 cloves garlic, very finely sliced
2 red chillies, deseeded and finely chopped
salt and freshly ground black pepper
2 x 400 g tins chickpeas, drained and rinsed
1 bunch spring onions, finely chopped
1 bunch coriander, parsley, mint or basil (about
   50 g in total)
juice of 1 lemon
250 g feta or goat's cheese, roughly chopped

1.   Heat half the olive oil and sweat the red onions and garlic for
      about 5 minutes, until soft. Add the red chillies and give it a
      stir. Allow to cool, then season very well with salt and pepper.
2.   In a large bowl, mix the onion and oil mixture with the
      chickpeas, spring onions and herbs. Add the lemon juice, mix
      well and season. Add some more of the remaining
      100 ml of olive oil if you want to make it more luscious and
      sloppy. Add the cheese and mix carefully. Check the seasoning
      again and serve.

Chickpea, feta

This is a perfect accompaniment to the coriander chicken (p. 45) but is also good as dinner by itself.

and coriander salad

Spaghetti with rich onion, thyme and garlic sauce

Serves 2

When cooking pasta, I usually drain it and rinse in plenty of water, often from a boiled kettle. This helps get rid of the starch, which can cause it to clump together. I'm sure I'm gravely insulting my Italian brother-in-law by doing this, but once it's rinsed, I put it back in the saucepan, add a good splash of olive oil and season the pasta well. It's then perfectly warm, seasoned and ready for whatever sauce I have in mind.

With regards to portion sizes for pasta, and spaghetti in particular, I always get it wrong. Not that I mind leftovers, as it can be a good school lunch the next day if mixed with some pesto. I normally allow 100 g to 120 g of pasta per person, depending on how savage you feel.

4 or 5 tbsp olive oil
2 large onions, very thinly sliced
1 head garlic, all the cloves peeled and crushed
1 or 2 glasses white wine
a few sprigs of thyme
salt and freshly ground black pepper
about 250 g spaghetti (half a pack)
grated Parmesan, to serve
chopped flat-leaf parsley, to garnish

1. Heat the olive oil in a large frying pan and gently sauté the onions until soft and just starting to colour. If you do this slow enough, it will take about 15 minutes. Chuck in the garlic, white wine and thyme and season well. Turn up the heat and cook off the wine. When most of the liquid has evaporated, remove from the heat and keep warm while you cook the pasta according to the packet instructions.
2. When the pasta is ready, drain it and rinse with a kettle full of boiling water. Return the pasta to the big saucepan, splash with some olive oil and season well. Serve with some of the onion sauce and top with plenty of black pepper and Parmesan and garnish with chopped parsley.

Grilled mackerel with marinated cucumber and mustard crème fraîche

Serves 4

4 mackerel fillets
a knob of butter or a splash of olive oil
salt and freshly ground black pepper

for the marinated cucumber:
100 ml white wine vinegar
1 bay leaf
1 red chilli, finely chopped, with or without seeds
2 tbsp caster sugar
1 big cucumber
1 small onion or a couple shallots, finely chopped
1 bunch chives, finely chopped
salt and freshly ground black pepper

for the mustard crème fraîche:
1 small tub crème fraîche (about 170 g)
1 small bunch dill, finely chopped
1 tbsp Dijon or wholegrain mustard

1. To make the marinated cucumber, heat the vinegar in a small saucepan with the bay leaf, chilli and caster sugar. Bring to the boil, then strain the liquid and allow to cool. If you wanted to be good, you should salt the cucumber to remove excess liquid. I never bother, so just peel the cucumber, slice thinly and mix with the chilli and vinegar syrup, the onion and chopped chives. Season to taste and set aside.
2. Turn up your grill to high and dot the mackerel skin with some butter or a drizzle of olive oil and some salt and pepper. Grill the fish skin side up until the skin starts to bubble, blister and char. It really does cook very quickly – maybe 2 to 3 minutes.
3. Mix the crème fraîche with the dill and mustard.
4. Serve the fish with a spoonful of cucumber and a dollop of the mustard crème fraîche.

Grilled
mackerel

Onion broth with cheese and garlic toast

Serves 4

For a fabulous French onion soup, you need fabulous stock of the chicken and/or beef variety. Most commercial stock cubes are full of rubbish, so either buy decent ones (like the Marigold powdered stock, which you can get in health food stores) or forget about the stock cube and just get a bit more enthusiastic with the salt and pepper, herbs and garlic!

a good knob of butter
4 large white onions, finely sliced
1 tsp sugar
salt and freshly ground black pepper
a splash of brandy (optional)
a few sprigs of thyme
1 bay leaf

1 litre stock or water
2 tbsp soy sauce
1 or 2 tbsp Worcestershire sauce
4 slices sourdough bread
4 cloves garlic, peeled
a drizzle of olive oil
150 g grated Gruyère cheese

1. Melt the butter in a large, heavy-based saucepan and slowly sweat the onions until soft and flaccid. You aren't looking for colour, just really soft onions. When they are pretty sad and limp looking, turn up the heat, add in the sugar and season well. When they are just starting to colour, add the brandy and keep cooking on a high heat so that the alcohol cooks off. Add the herbs and slowly add the stock, stirring constantly, then add the soy and Worcestershire sauces. Bring up to the boil, then reduce the heat and simmer gently for about 10 minutes.

2. Toast or grill the bread, then rub the garlic cloves onto each slice of bread. It's almost like you're using the bread as a grater for the garlic. If you do it well, you should be left with pathetic little stumps of garlic, which you can then chuck into the soup. Drizzle the garlic toasts with a small bit of olive oil, then top with the grated cheese and grill until the cheese is bubbling and melted. Set aside.

3. Now taste the soup. If it tastes bland and watery, keep cooking to reduce it down and intensify the flavours. Add more soy sauce or another teaspoon of sugar or salt and pepper. Check it again, then spoon into bowls. Gently place the cheesy toast on top and serve.

53

Poached haddock an

Poached haddock and egg with parsnip purée

Serves 4

This sounds like a lot of work, but feel free to ditch the haddock, just make the parsnip purée and serve with a poached egg and a handful of greens for a comfort dinner at its best.

1 kg parsnips (about 3 big parsnips)
salt and freshly ground black pepper
a few sprigs of thyme
2 tbsp crème fraîche
1 tbsp Dijon mustard
a few good knobs of butter
4 smoked haddock fillets (about 150 g each)
a splash of milk
4 poached eggs
watercress or baby spinach, to serve

1. Peel and roughly chop the parsnips. Place in a large saucepan of cold water, add a good pinch of salt and the thyme, then bring to the boil. Reduce to a simmer and cook for about 15 minutes, or until the parsnip chunks are soft. Drain and ditch the thyme.
2. Get a blender or food processor out and add the parsnips, crème fraîche, mustard and butter. Whizz until smooth by pulsing it often rather than turning it into baby food. You're making a purée, not a smoothie. Put it back in a small saucepan and add another knob of butter. Check the seasoning and reheat when you're about to serve.
3. In a frying pan, bring enough water to cover the fish and a splash of milk to the boil. Add the haddock fillets and gently simmer for about 5 to 10 minutes. Drain.
4. Serve the haddock with a big spoonful of the parsnip purée and a poached egg on top. Garnish with watercress or baby spinach. If you want to be very decadent, heat up some cream, add a heaped tablespoon of wholegrain mustard and pour it on top.

Tag bol

Serves 4 to 6

Who doesn't love spag bol? (OK, vegetarians can skip that question.) Who doesn't love garlic bread? (All hands should be raised at this stage.) Now I know everyone can make garlic bread, but this is the quickest and healthiest version of garlic bread you can make. All you need is fabulous bread (and fabulous garlic, olive oil and salt, of course). And finally, unbeknownst to many of us, the trick to a really good spag bol is to add some chicken liver to enrich the sauce and to make it with white wine (rather than red) and some cream. You could add diced carrot and celery, but I really prefer to leave it plain and let the white wine and chicken livers work their magic. It works well with tagliatelle, hence its new name: tag bol.

2 onions, finely chopped

a good knob of butter

6 Portobello mushrooms, very finely diced

4 cloves garlic, peeled and crushed

600 g minced beef

100 g chicken livers

½ bottle white wine

a couple of bay leaves

salt and freshly ground black pepper

1 x 700 g jar passata

250 ml cream

a little freshly grated nutmeg

500 g tagliatelle or papparadelle

1 bunch flat-leaf parsley, to garnish

garlic bread (p. 57), to serve

1. In a sturdy saucepan, fry the onions in the butter until soft but not coloured. Add the mushrooms and garlic. Add the mince in chunks and break it up with a wooden spoon, incorporating the meat rather than just dumping the whole lot in. Add the chicken livers, half the wine and the bay leaves. It will look horrid, but have faith. Keep the heat up high and gradually cook off most of the wine so that it looks quite dry. Season well, then add the passata. Stir well and bring back up to simmering. Leave it on a very low heat, cover with a lid and let it cook gently for 1 hour, stirring occasionally.

2. Add the cream and nutmeg and cook for another hour on a low heat. Check the seasoning. It should be a gorgeous red brick colour as opposed to bright red.

3. Cook the pasta according to the packet instructions. Drain, rinse and toss with some olive oil or a knob of butter. Season and toss with the sauce and garnish with the parsley. Serve with garlic bread (p. 57).

Garlic bread

Makes 1 loaf

1 loaf of excellent white or sourdough bread, sliced
4 to 8 cloves garlic, peeled
olive oil
Maldon sea salt

1. Toast the bread really well. While still hot, rub the garlic up and down each slice so that it gets 'grated' onto the toast. I use about three-quarters of a clove on each piece of bread. Chuck the leftover bits of garlic into the bol sauce on p. 56 if you're making this to serve with it.
2. Drizzle the slices of toast with generous (but not crazy) amounts of olive oil and sprinkle with Maldon salt (or some other posh sea salt). Don't use rubbishy salt on this, as it will taste far too salty.

Daube of pork with apricots

Serves 4 to 6

You can make this a very long-winded Michelin star way or else keep it easy and snappy, like I've tried to do here.

a splash of sunflower oil
1 kg fillet of pork or boned pork shoulder
salt and freshly ground black pepper
2 onions, roughly chopped
500 ml red wine
500 ml vegetable or chicken stock or water
1 or 2 heads garlic, cloves peeled and roughly chopped
200 ml olive oil
1 x 400 g tin tomatoes
12 dried apricots
a pinch of mustard seeds, fennel seeds and coriander seeds
a few sprigs of thyme

1. Preheat the oven to 180°C.
2. Heat the oil in a large ovenproof saucepan and cut the pork into large chunks. Brown the pork until golden brown in colour and season well. Add the onions and continue to brown, then deglaze the pan with the wine and the stock or water.
3. Add the rest of the ingredients. Bring up to the boil, cover with a lid or tin foil and transfer the pot to the oven to cook for 2 hours. After about 1 hour, I usually remove the lid so that the cooking juice starts to reduce and you get a really concentrated flavour. The pork should be super tender. Check the seasoning and reduce the cooking liquor further in a saucepan before serving, if necessary.

Beans and bacon

Serves 2

This is very popular in our household. Feel free to up the herb, chilli and garlic quotient as much as you like. It nearly looks too dull and boring to bother making, but it really does taste good. If you use chorizo, the oil will make it go a horrid pink colour (like in the photo)!

splash of olive oil

1 onion, diced

a pinch of caster sugar

200 g lardons, bacon or chorizo, finely diced

2 cloves garlic

1 glass white wine

1 x 400 g tin flageolet beans, drained and rinsed

2 heaped tbsp crème fraîche

a sprig of thyme

a pinch of chilli flakes

freshly ground black pepper

green salad, to serve

crusty bread, to serve

grated Parmesan, to serve

1. Heat the olive oil in a pan and fry the onion for a few minutes, until soft and starting to colour. Add the sugar and the bacon. Fry until crispy, then turn down the heat and add the garlic. Add the wine to deglaze the pan, then add the rest of the ingredients. Mix gently and simmer for a few minutes until well mixed and piping hot. Season with loads of black pepper. I rarely add salt, as the bacon gives it plenty of flavour. This is perfect with a green salad and served on a hunk of nice bread. It also tastes good with a sprinkle of Parmesan.

Super-healthy salmon and tuna fishcakes

Super-healthy salmon and tuna fishcakes

Serves 4 as a starter or 2 as a main

Don't stress out if you can't get lime leaves or anything else off the list. Just add more of everything else. Also, if you ever do come across lime leaves, buy a bunch of them, wrap them up well in cling film and freeze them. The same goes for the lemongrass – it's not ideal, but it works OK as they can be hard to find when you need them.

2 red onions, diced
2 red chillies, deseeded and diced
2 lime leaves
1 stalk lemongrass
juice of 2 limes
1 small bunch coriander
1 small bunch basil
a knob of ginger, peeled
2 tbsp tamari or soy sauce

1 tsp fish sauce
a splash of sesame oil
200 g fresh salmon fillet, skin removed and roughly chopped
200 g fresh tuna fillet, skin removed and roughly chopped
a handful of sesame seeds
sweet chilli sauce (p. 62), to serve

1. Preheat the oven to 200°C. Line a baking tray with parchment paper.
2. Whizz all the ingredients except the fish and sesame seeds together in a food processor until smooth. Add the fish and pulse so that it's processed but not mushy baby food. Shape the fish into balls and place on the baking tray. If you can, chill for 10 minutes.
3. Sprinkle with sesame seeds, then bake for 10 to 12 minutes. If you can, gently turn them over halfway through so they can brown on both sides. They do cook quite quickly, and you may like to serve them a bit rare inside. Let them settle for a minute before removing from the paper (they are quite delicate, as there is no egg to bind them), then serve with sweet chilli sauce.

Sweet chilli sauce

Makes 500 ml

Yes, there's quite a bit of sugar in here, but a lot less than in commercial varieties. Stored in a jar in your fridge, this should keep for a few weeks, no problem.

2 cloves garlic
1 chilli, with seeds
1 red pepper, with seeds – just the stalk removed
1 stalk lemongrass
a knob of ginger
a few lime leaves (optional)
200 ml water
50 ml white wine vinegar
50 g sugar
salt
1 bunch coriander, stalks and leaves separated

1.   Put everything except the coriander leaves in a pot. Bring to the boil, then let it simmer for approximately 45 minutes, until jammy. Remove from the heat and blend until pretty smooth. Once cool, add in the chopped coriander leaves.

Yes, there's quite a bit of sugar in here, but a lot less than in commercial varieties. Stored in a jar in your fridge, this should keep for a few weeks, no problem.

Barley and root vegetable stew

Serves 4 to 6

This barley and veg soup is a kind of 'chicken noodle soup for the soul', but without the chicken. I always associate barley with the oxtail soup my mum used to make 10 million years ago. When I did a little research about barley, I was surprised and delighted to find that it had a decent amount of vitamin B6 and iron in it. Also, within Islamic traditions, it was prescribed as a medicine to help people cope with the death of loved ones. When you taste barley cooked lovingly in a simple broth, it's not hard to imagine the comfort it can provide.

We use the pricey but nice Marigold stock in all the soups we sell in itsa, the reasons being that it's not full of rubbish like MSG and it's vegetarian. Check out the labels on stocks in your supermarket versus products you find in a health food store. Look for ones that make better reading. Feel free to add a few cloves of garlic to this, as I'm convinced it helps keep flu at bay.

a good splash of olive oil
1 large onion, chopped
2 leeks, chopped into 2 cm pieces
2 big carrots, chopped
2 parsnips, chopped
1 turnip, chopped
1 heaped tbsp Marigold vegetable stock
800 ml water
110 g pearl barley
salt and freshly ground black pepper
warm bread, to serve

1.	Heat the olive oil in a big saucepan and sauté the onion until golden brown. Add the leeks, carrots, parsnips and turnips. Cover and cook for a few minutes, until starting to soften ever so slightly.
2.	Mix the stock in a cup with a small amount of boiling water to get all the lumps out, then add to the saucepan. Add the 800 ml water and the barley. Stir well.
3.	Bring up to the boil, then cover and simmer gently for about 1 hour. Check the seasoning. Serve in big bowls with lovely warm bread.

Lemon and garlic
poached chicken

Lemon and garlic poached chicken

Serves 4 to 6

This is my kind of dish: rustic, not too creamy and full of garlic. A great dinner dish for informal fun, although having a good-sized heavy-based saucepan or casserole dish makes this easier to do in one go. Use legs, thighs, breasts or ask your butcher to joint a whole chicken for you into 6 pieces, leaving you with 2 breasts, thighs and legs. You'll also have 2 wings, but they're too skimpy to serve on their own. This recipe appears in plenty of cookbooks, including ones from Tom Kime and Rachel Allen. It's a classic.

2 tbsp olive oil
approx. 8 chicken pieces, on the bone
salt and freshly ground black pepper
approx. 20 cloves garlic, unpeeled
250 ml white wine
zest and juice of 2 lemons
a few sprigs of thyme
2 bay leaves
500 ml stock
1 baguette, sliced
fresh chopped parsley, to serve

1. Heat the olive oil in a big saucepan and brown the chicken on all sides for about 5 minutes, until golden brown. Make sure you get a good colour on it at this stage or it will end up pale and anaemic. Season well on all sides. When the chicken is good and brown, just quickly transfer it onto a plate and discard all the oil in the pan. There will be quite a lot of fat here and it's good to get rid of it now.
2. Add the garlic, wine, lemon zest and juice, herbs and stock to the saucepan and give everything a good stir. Carefully put the chicken back in the cooking liquor to simmer gently for about 25 minutes.
3. Meanwhile, toast some baguette slices and have them piled on a plate.
4. When the chicken is cooked, remove some of the garlic cloves, squeeze them from their skins and spread onto the baguette slices. Transfer the chicken into big bowls and add some garlicky baguette slices. Sprinkle with parsley, spoon over some of the cooking juices and serve.

Chickpea, sweet potato and chorizo stew

Serves 4

I love this dish and we serve it a lot in one of our cafés. If you're a vegetarian, you can leave out the chorizo and it will be just as tasty, especially if you add a pinch of smoked sweet paprika, which gives a lovely, meaty taste.

a few knobs of butter

3 or 4 sweet potatoes, sliced into
   2 cm-thick pieces

500 ml water

1 tbsp honey

salt and freshly ground black pepper

a splash of olive oil

1 onion, chopped

1 tsp cumin seed

1 tsp coriander seed

1 or 2 chorizo sausages, roughly
   chopped

a good squeeze of tomato purée

2 x 400 g tins chickpeas, drained and
   rinsed

1 x 400 g tin chopped tomatoes

pinch of sugar

100 g baby spinach

crusty bread, to serve

a handful of coriander, chopped,
   to serve

1. Heat the butter in a large frying pan. Fry the sweet potatoes on each side, until they're starting to caramelise. Add the water and the honey. Season well and cook over a medium heat, until the potatoes are starting to get tender – about 15 minutes. You may have to add more water if it cooks off too quickly, but when they're cooked, most of the water should have cooked off. Set aside.

2. Meanwhile, in a large saucepan, heat the olive oil and fry the onion along with the cumin and coriander seed for a few minutes. Add the chorizo and let it cook and start to brown at the edges for a good 5 minutes. Add the tomato purée, chickpeas, tinned tomatoes and sugar and cook for another 5 to 10 minutes.

3. Add the spinach and stir so that the spinach wilts. Add the sweet potatoes and any juices left in the pan, mixing carefully so that the potatoes don't break up. Serve in bowls along with good bread and fresh coriander leaves.

Lamb and chickpea soupy stew

Serves 4 to 6

I sometimes don't bother making dishes like this as often as I should because I reckon they'll be a tad dull, but the combo of cloves and paprika works a treat. Lamb shoulder is cheap as chips but can be quite fatty, so trim it up well or ask the butcher to give you something leaner but still suitable for braising. I think pork or beef would also work really well in this stew, although the lamb is great with chickpeas.

2 tbsp olive oil
2 onions, chopped
4 cloves garlic, chopped
600 g diced lamb shoulder
salt and freshly ground black pepper
2 tsp ground cumin
1 tsp paprika
½ tsp ground cloves
2 bay leaves

a good squeeze of tomato purée
1 litre chicken stock
3 x 400 g tins chickpeas
2 x 400 g tins tomatoes
1 bunch coriander, chopped,
 to garnish
black olives, to garnish
crusty bread, to serve
green salad, to serve

1. Heat the olive oil in a big saucepan, one for which you have some sort of lid. Sweat the onions and garlic for 5 minutes, until soft, then turn up the heat and chuck in the lamb. Brown the lamb, but try not to let the mixture burn. Season well, then add in the cumin, paprika, cloves and bay leaves. Mix well so the spices coat all the lamb. Add in the tomato purée and mix well, then add in the stock, chickpeas and tomatoes.

2. Put the lid on and cook for about 3 hours over a very gentle heart. My lid was a bit dodgy, so I ended up topping it up with another 500 ml water, but see how you go. Taste and adjust the seasoning. Garnish with coriander and olives, and serve with bread and salad.

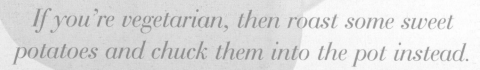

If you're vegetarian, then roast some sweet potatoes and chuck them into the pot instead.

Quick Asian noodle supper

Serves 4 to 6

The list of ingredients may seem long, but most of them are store cupboard bits and bobs. This one-pot dish is comforting and tasty. I sometimes chuck in frozen prawns, but chicken would do. You can use fresh prawns too, just be sensible about cooking times. If they're raw, allow a little more time, and if using cooked meat, just chuck it in at the end so that it heats through. Or else leave the meat out altogether and add more veg, such as bok choy.

2 tbsp olive oil
3 onions, chopped
3 cloves garlic, chopped
2 stalks lemongrass, finely chopped
a big knob of ginger, peeled and
    finely chopped
3 tbsp miso paste
8 Portobello mushrooms, finely sliced
2 litres water

2 tbsp fish sauce
2 tbsp soy sauce
2 tbsp sweet chilli sauce
250 g rice noodles
300 g prawns
2 bunches spring onions, roughly
    chopped
1 head of bok choy, roughly chopped
1 bunch coriander, roughly chopped

1. Heat the olive oil and sweat the onions with the garlic, lemongrass and ginger. Add the miso paste and stir well. If it starts to burn, chuck in a splash of water. Add the mushrooms and mix well before adding the water and three sauces. Bring up to a gentle simmer and taste. You may want to gently cook for 10 minutes to allow the flavours to develop, but feel free to add a bit more seasoning by way of fish, soy or chilli sauce.

2. Break the rice noodles in half and chuck in. Check your packet instructions for the recommended cooking times for them, but they should be able to cook in the soup. Add the remaining ingredients, and when the prawns and noodles are cooked, serve in big bowls.

Duck dal supper

Duck dal supper

Serves 2 very generously

When mung beans are dehusked, they're called moong dal (amongst other names) and are used a lot in Asian cooking. I'd never cooked them at home until I came across this Simon Hopkinson recipe. Since making it, it's become a firm favourite and is often cooked minus the duck legs.

2 duck legs

olive oil

salt and freshly ground black pepper

1 onion, finely chopped

6 cloves garlic, sliced

1 tsp ground cumin

a pinch of chilli flakes

40 g butter

300 g moong dal, rinsed well

500 ml vegetable stock or water

rind of 2 lemons, chopped

1 big bunch mint, roughly chopped

1.   Preheat the oven to 180°C.

2.   Fry the duck legs with a splash of olive oil in a heavy-based saucepan that can also go into the oven and that you have a lid for. Fry well on all sides till golden brown and season well. Remove the duck legs from the pan, set aside and chuck out all but 1 tablespoon of fat.

3.   Fry the onions and garlic till they are just starting to colour, then add the cumin, chilli flakes and butter. The butter gives it great richness, but if you want to leave it out, do. Add the rinsed dal and mix well so it gets coated with the flavours. Add the stock (or water plus extra salt) and bring up to the boil. Add the lemon rind and mint and stir well, then place the duck legs into the pan.

4.   Cover with the lid and cook for 40 minutes in the oven. Remove from the oven but keep the lid on for 10 minutes before opening it and mixing the dal lightly. Check the seasoning, garnish with more mint or some basil and serve.

Fish pie

Serves 6 to 8 hungry blokes, possibly 10 ladylike guests

I endeavoured to make the simplest, laziest and tastiest fish pie in less than 30 minutes. And you know what? It was very manageable and super tasty. It fed eight people, the wash-up was minimal and everyone's plate was clean.

I'm leaving it up to you what fish or shellfish you want to use. I used smoked cod, haddock and salmon, none of which I poached, but all of which the fishmonger had already skinned. Scallops, prawns and mussels would all be delicious additions. Serve with a big spoonful of buttery peas and enjoy.

100 g butter
150 g flour
1 litre milk
1 tbsp Dijon mustard
1 glass white wine
salt and freshly ground black pepper
1 massive bunch parsley, roughly
   chopped

1.5 kg skinned fish or prepared
   shellfish
2 kg spuds, peeled
a few knobs of butter
250 g cheddar, grated
cooked peas, to serve

1.   Preheat the oven to 200°C.
2.   Melt the butter in a saucepan and add the flour to make a roux. Don't let it burn, but do cook it over a gentle heat for at least 3 minutes to cook out the flour. It will look like dough. Gradually whisk in the milk. Lumps will come and go, but a whisk sorts this out. Add the Dijon mustard and white wine. Check the seasoning and add in the parsley. The smoked fish will make it pretty salty, but make sure your béchamel still has good flavour. Add in your fish and mix well. The sauce will still be pretty hot, so you'll be able to mix the fish in very easily. Set aside for a few minutes while you finish off the spuds.
3.   Chop the spuds into small chunks and put in a large saucepan of cold water. Bring up to the boil and cook until tender. Drain and put back in the pot with a tea towel on top. This helps them to go light and fluffy when mashed. Add the butter and mash quickly and roughly, then mix in the cheese. Season very lightly.
4.   Pour the fish mix into a large gratin dish and top with a layer of mashed spuds. Bake for about 45 minutes, until the top is golden brown, then allow to settle for 10 minutes. Serve with peas.

Fish pie

Beef rendang

Serves 6 to 8

These are very easygoing flavours. Kids to grannies will eat this Asian beef stew, which isn't killer spicy, but is aromatic enough to be a bit of a treat.

4 cloves

1 cinnamon stick

1 tbsp coriander seeds

1 tsp cumin seeds

1 tsp turmeric

a good pinch of dried chillies

a few glugs of olive oil

2 onions, chopped

6 cloves garlic, peeled and sliced

2 stalks lemongrass, finely chopped

a big knob of ginger, peeled and sliced

2 kg chuck or rump steak

salt and freshly ground black pepper

1 tbsp soft brown sugar

2 x 400 g tins coconut milk

1 bunch coriander, chopped

boiled rice, to serve

1. Put all the spices in a large saucepan and gently heat for 1 minute to dry roast them. Either grind them up or pour into a cup and crush them with the end of a rolling pin. Pour the crushed spices back into the saucepan and add the olive oil. Add the onion, garlic, lemongrass and ginger and sweat for a few minutes. Add in the meat and mix well so it's coated in the spices. Season well with salt and pepper and add the sugar. You can turn the heat up and if the meat browns a little, great – but don't caramelise the meat at the expense of burning the spices! Add the coconut milk.

2. Cook for at least 2 hours on a very gentle heat. I didn't keep a lid on it as I wanted it to reduce, but do give it the occasional stir, as it tends to burn the bottom of the pan. Eventually the meat should be incredibly tender and the sauce nice and thick. Adjust the seasoning and serve with loads of chopped coriander and some boiled rice. This is one of those dishes that also tastes very good the next day. If it has dried out too much upon reheating, just add a few splashes of water and check the seasoning.

Baked aubergines with tomato, Parmesan and crème fraîche

Perfect supper for 2 to 3

This is quite rich, but is absolutely delicious. I'm often stuck with aubergines in the fridge at the end of the week and forget to cook them until I remember how much I love this vegetarian treat. The key is to reduce the tomato sauce and the crème fraîche so that you get wildly concentrated flavours.

1 x 400 g tin tomatoes
50 g butter
4 cloves garlic, thinly sliced
2 tsp caster sugar
1 bunch thyme or rosemary, leaves
   chopped
salt and freshly ground black pepper

2 aubergines, sliced into 2-cm-thick
   rounds
1 x 250 g tub crème fraîche
50 g Parmesan, finely grated
olive oil
crusty bread, to serve
green salad, to serve

1.   Put the tomatoes in a small saucepan along with the butter, garlic, sugar, herbs and seasoning. Bring to a simmer and cook for about 20 minutes over a gentle heat, until it's thicker than ketchup, stirring often with a wooden spoon as it can burn if you don't keep an eye on it.

2.   Meanwhile, sprinkle the aubergines generously with salt and lay them out on kitchen paper on a baking tray.

3.   In another saucepan, heat the crème fraîche until simmering and reduce by a third. It will start to look like curdled yoghurt, but don't worry. Take off the heat, mix in the Parmesan and set aside. Taste both the tomato sauce and the crème fraîche and make sure you're happy with the seasoning. You can do both these stages the night before if that's handier and just leave in your fridge until ready to assemble.

4.   Preheat the oven to 180°C. Wipe the salt off the aubergines and fry in batches in olive oil until golden on both sides. Don't bother seasoning them except with pepper. Drain on kitchen paper and allow to cool, then layer them in a gratin dish. Top with tomato sauce and then spoonfuls of the crème fraîche, which won't spread – merely drop it on top of the tomato sauce with a spoon. Bake for 25 to 30 minutes, until bubbling. Drizzle with more olive oil and let it rest for 10 minutes before serving with bread and a green salad.

Lazy fish soup

Lazy fish soup

Serves 4 very generously if eating on its own for dinner

I love eating a classic fish soup in a French bistro, but a great shellfish stock takes a lot of loving, which you need in order to make a really great fish soup. This recipe is a kind of soupy stew and doesn't involve bones, stock and hours of your time. It's lazy but tasty and satisfying and could easily be a meal in itself with the accoutrements. Feel free to play around with whatever fish you want to add.

3 tbsp olive oil
4 cloves garlic, chopped
2 onions, chopped
2 leeks, chopped
1 fennel, diced
½ head celery, chopped
1 bay leaf
½ tsp cayenne pepper
a good splash of Tabasco
a good splash of Worcestershire sauce
a pinch of dried chilli flakes

2 x 400 g tins chopped tomatoes
a good pinch of sugar
1 litre vegetable stock
zest and juice of 1 orange
salt and freshly ground black pepper
500 g monkfish, cut into chunks
200 g frozen prawns (optional)
200 g mussels
chopped parsley
rouille (p. 78), to serve
Parmesan croûtes (p. 78), to serve

1. Heat the olive oil in a big, heavy saucepan and sweat the garlic and onions till soft. Add the leeks, fennel, celery, bay leaf and spices. Mix well and sweat for a few minutes, until well coated with the spices. Add the tomatoes, sugar, stock, orange juice and zest.

2. Cook on a gentle heat for about 45 minutes to let the flavours develop. Taste and season with salt and pepper. You can cool it down and refrigerate it at this stage, or else chuck in the fish and cook for another 10 minutes on a gentle heat. Make sure the mussels are well rinsed and scrubbed before you put them in and that they are fully closed. After cooking for 10 minutes, discard any mussels that haven't opened up. Scatter some chopped parsley on top and serve with the rouille and Parmesan croûtes below for a perfect and complete dinner.

Rouille

Makes approx. 350 ml

2 egg yolks, at room temperature
approx. 250 ml olive oil
3 cloves garlic, crushed
2 tbsp stale breadcrumbs
a good pinch of cayenne pepper
a good squeeze of tomato purée
a few sprigs of fresh thyme, leaves finely chopped
salt

1. Whisk together the egg yolks with a few drops of olive oil. Gradually and very slowly add the oil. When the mixture has started to thicken, you can add it a bit more quickly. After adding about 150 ml oil, add the rest of the ingredients and taste. You may want to add the rest of the olive oil, or you may prefer to keep the rouille thicker and stronger. It will make too much just to serve with the fish soup on p. 77, but I love eating this anyway with char-grilled vegetables.

Parmesan croûtes

1 small baguette
olive oil
2 cloves garlic, peeled
50 to 100 g grated Parmesan

1. Preheat the oven to 160°C.
2. Slice the baguette into 2-cm-thick slices and lay out on a baking tray. Brush generously with olive oil and bake for 15 to 20 minutes, until golden brown. Once they're a good colour, remove from the oven and allow them to cool, then rub with a whole garlic clove for extra flavour. You can then sprinkle them with Parmesan and heat them again so that the Parmesan melts, or else just serve the croûtes with the soup on p. 77 and sprinkle the Parmesan directly into the soup along with some parsley, lots of black pepper and a blob of rouille.

Smoked haddock chowder

Serves 4 to 6

This serves 4 to 6, depending on how much fish you put in. Feel free to add prawns, mussels, salmon or any fish you fancy. If you add less milk at the end, you could just top with mash potatoes and make a fish pie. This is the only time that I mean it when I say that the garlic is optional. It was genuinely a bit overpowering, but I threw it in anyway for medicinal purposes.

400 to 600 g smoked haddock
400 ml milk
1 bay leaf
a few sprigs of thyme
a knob of butter
2 leeks, finely chopped
2 cloves garlic, crushed (optional)
2 carrots, diced
2 medium potatoes, diced
½ head celery, diced
1 heaped tsp mild curry powder
300 ml vegetable stock
50 ml cream
salt and freshly ground black pepper

1. Cook the haddock in the milk with the bay leaf and thyme in a small saucepan. Gently bring to the boil, then turn off the heat and leave it alone for 20 minutes while you get the veg prepped.

2. Heat a big knob of butter in a frying pan and sweat the leeks and garlic for a few minutes before adding the carrots, potatoes, celery and curry powder. Mix well. When you can really smell the curry powder, add the stock and slowly bring to a gentle simmer. Cook for 10 minutes, until the vegetables are soft.

3. Meanwhile, remove the skin from the haddock and set aside chunks of fish. Strain the milk and pour into a jug. Add the cream to the soup and about half the milk. Add the haddock and cook for 5 minutes over a gentle heat and taste. Add more milk and adjust the seasoning, but don't boil the heck out of this dish or it will look slightly curdled and will toughen up the flavours. It's OK to let it cool and reheat it the next day, but I think it tastes better if made and served straight away.

Bit on the Side 4

I'm one of those wannabe do-gooders that gets a box of veg delivered each week and it's always a bit of a Russian roulette in terms of what we'll end up with from week to week. As a result, there are always vegetables of varying degrees of health kicking around, along with end-of-the-world supplies of tinned tomatoes, lentils, barley and various beans and packets of dried pasta. As long as there are garlic cloves, olive oil and a bit of Parmesan, you can always get fed in our house.

But going to a good veg shop and making the vegetables shine at dinner is a win-win situation. You're getting more of your five a day, you can splash out on making something a bit fancier without spending a fortune *and* you're doing your bit for the environment by eating less meat! And as good as I try to be about eating seasonally – if the truth be told, I'm probably not that good – every now and then I have to break out and cook something that tastes of sunshine, like the roasted red peppers with halloumi (p. 96).

If you're a reluctant or lazy shopper (like me), a good staple to consider stocking up on is frozen veg, namely peas, broad beans, soy beans and artichoke hearts. Frozen artichokes are really great to cook with because the tinned ones are too soggy and briny for my liking and the ones in oil are just too greasy when heated up. The frozen ones are dead handy. I fry them on a high heat straight from frozen in some olive oil with a ton of garlic until they just start to colour. Then I add a good squeeze of lemon juice, a few bits of thyme and toss them with some pasta, Parmesan and some more olive oil. It's a really tasty and quick supper. Frozen peas are also perfect fodder served on some mashed potatoes with a soft fried egg. Ultimate comfort and ease!

It's fair to say that the dishes in this chapter, despite being called bits on the side, are definitely star attractions.

Fennel salad

Serves 6 to 8 as a side

Have everything ready to be sliced and mixed together, as the fennel and radish can start to look a little grim if they don't get mixed with some acid (which comes from the lemon juice). Once it's mixed it'll look fine for a few hours, but like all salads, it's better made closer to the time of consumption, rather than sitting around gradually getting soggy and discoloured.

juice of 2 small lemons or 1 orange
4 tbsp olive oil
1 tsp honey
4 fennel bulbs, thinly sliced
2 yellow peppers, skinned and finely sliced
1 bunch radishes (about 100 g), thinly sliced
½ head celery, chopped
1 small bunch chives or spring onions, roughly chopped
salt and freshly ground black pepper

1. Mix the juice, olive oil and honey together. Chuck everything else into a bowl, mix with the dressing and season well.

Note: I love to thinly slice fennel and drizzle it with some sherry vinegar, olive oil, soy sauce, toasted sesame seeds and agave syrup for a delicious Asian-style salad that's ready in no time.

Pomegranate and green bean salad

Serves 4 to 6 as a side

The Ottolenghi cookbook is one of my favourites and their vegetable and salad dishes always provide fresh ideas for unusual combinations, like this salad below.

for the salad:
450 g green beans
1 red onion, thinly sliced
1 pomegranate
1 small bunch flat-leaf parsley, chopped
1 small bunch mint, chopped

for the dressing:
150 ml olive oil
50 ml white wine vinegar
1 clove garlic, chopped
2 tbsp honey
1 tsp Dijon mustard
salt and freshly ground black pepper

1.   Blanch the beans for 1 minute, then drain and refresh in cold water.
2.   Firmly thud the whole pomegranates against a wooden chopping board until you feel the inside flesh go soft and mushy, then cut it in half and squeeze out the seeds into a bowl. Discard any of the yellowish pith. Add the beans and herbs to the bowl.
3.   Whisk all the dressing ingredients together and toss the whole lot together.

Pomegranate and green bean salad

Char-grilled broccoli with lemon, chilli and garlic

Serves 4 to 6

I'm normally pretty reluctant to pull out my char-grill pan for anything less than a nice steak, but it does work wonders on sad, fridge-lagged vegetables like broccoli and cauliflower.

Asparagus are made for the grill, especially if you give them the same blanching, refreshing, char-grilled treatment that the broccoli gets in this recipe; you'll find all they need is a simple splash of olive oil or melted butter, some sea salt, pepper and loads of Parmesan.

2 heads broccoli (approx. 1 kg)
100 ml olive oil
6 cloves garlic, thinly sliced
2 red chillies, deseeded and thinly sliced
salt and freshly ground black pepper
juice of 1 lemon

1. Separate the broccoli into little florets and have a colander ready in your sink. Bring a large pot of water to the boil and cook the broccoli for just 1 minute. Drain and rinse in plenty of cold water, until the florets are cold. Drain well and put in the fridge to cool down and dry off further.
2. Meanwhile, heat half the olive oil in a small saucepan with the garlic and chillies. Cook gently for a few minutes, until the garlic is soft, and set aside.
3. When the broccoli is dry, toss in a bowl with the remaining olive oil and plenty of salt and pepper. Heat a char-grill pan or heavy-based frying pan until smoking and grill the broccoli in batches until nicely charred in parts. Put them back into a large mixing bowl, and when they're all done, toss with the lemon juice and the chilli and garlic oil. This tastes great when served warm or at room temperature, but doesn't take kindly to being left in the fridge overnight.

Braised Baby Gems

Serves 4 to 6 as a side

Cooked lettuce? Are you mad? Give it a go. Sometimes the leaves of the little Baby Gems are so tight that they seem reluctant to be made into a Caesar salad, so I teach them a lesson and cook the heck out of 'em for kicks. This dish only takes a few minutes to cook and is a tasty side dish that even the childer like.

4 heads Baby Gems
50 g butter
a good splash of olive oil
100 ml water
a few sprigs of thyme
2 cloves garlic, crushed
salt and freshly ground black pepper

1. Slice the Baby Gems in half lengthways. If some outer leaves fall off, so be it: don't bother cooking them.
2. Heat the butter and olive oil until foaming and fry the Baby Gems, flat side down, for about 1 minute, or until they are just starting to colour in parts. Add the water, thyme and garlic and season very well. Cook on a high heat for another minute. Baste the lettuces or turn them over gently and serve with a small bit of the garlicky, buttery cooking liquid.

Crunchy cucumber salad

Serves 4

This turns a boring old cucumber into something a lot more tasty.

½ loaf sourdough bread or small baguette, cut into cubes

50 ml olive oil

2 tbsp red wine vinegar

a few splashes of Tabasco sauce

2 cloves garlic, crushed

salt and freshly ground black pepper

1 large cucumber, roughly chopped into chunks

1 red onion, finely diced

1 x 250 g punnet cherry tomatoes, halved

100 g pitted black olives

2 tbsp toasted nuts, roughly chopped (hazelnuts work well)

1 small bunch flat-leaf parsley, roughly chopped

1. Toast the chunks of bread in an oven at 150°C until golden brown. Allow to cool fully.
2. Whisk the olive oil, vinegar, Tabasco and garlic together. Season well. Mix the remaining ingredients together and add the dressing. Mix well and serve.

Pasta salad with sage, sweet potato and halloumi

Serves 4 as a main

I have an unhealthy obsession with halloumi and spend too much time trying to get our chefs to use it, but most of the boy chefs think it's just one step away from tofu and regularly ignore my pleas to cook with it. A few of the girl chefs in our company are partial to it, so maybe it's a girl or Greek thing. Thick slices fried in butter till golden brown (and as soft as this rubbery cheese ever gets) can be heaven. Try frying it with lardons of bacon and adding a few handfuls of peas and crème fraîche for a really tasty pasta sauce.

Pasta salads (along with cold soups) usually give me the willies. However, the flavours here are rich and fabulous and the big pasta shells are a welcome respite from the array of flavours the rest of the recipe brings.

4 sweet potatoes
olive oil .
salt and freshly ground black pepper
400 g pasta shells
50 g butter
a handful of sage leaves
1 x 250 g pack halloumi

1. Preheat the oven to 180°C.
2. Peel the sweet potatoes and chop up roughly into chunks. Chuck them in a roasting tray, pour a few tablespoons of olive oil over them to coat and season well. Roast for about 45 minutes, until they're starting to caramelise and turn tender. Toss them around halfway through cooking so that they brown evenly.
3. Cook the pasta in boiling salted water until just tender. Drain and rinse well under cold water, then pour a bit of olive oil on the shells and mix well. The oil will stop the pasta from sticking together. Season lightly and set aside.

4. Gently melt the butter in a small saucepan, taking care that it doesn't get too hot, or it will brown and burn the sage leaves. Have a plate lined with kitchen paper nearby. Fry the sage leaves a few at a time for about 5 to 10 seconds, until crisp. Remove them carefully with a fork or tongs and drain on the kitchen paper.

5. Chop up the halloumi into small chunks and fry in a non-stick frying pan in 1 tablespoon of olive oil. This only takes a minute or two – all you want is for the halloumi to turn a golden colour. It's very hardy and won't melt or go gooey.

6. When the sweet potatoes are cooked, allow them to cool slightly, then toss with the pasta and halloumi. Season with more olive oil, if necessary, and plenty of black pepper. The halloumi is fairly salty, so go easy on the salt. Put the sage leaves on top and serve while still warm.

Beetroot and lentil vinaigrette

Serves 4 to 6

This is a lovely accompaniment to some goat's cheese grilled on top of a slice of thick toast. All it needs is some delicate peppery leaves, like rocket or mizuna, and maybe a splash of walnut or hazelnut oil. Serve with a big spoonful of this vinaigrette on top and enjoy.

2 large beetroot
olive oil
100 g Puy lentils
salt
250 ml red wine
1 red onion, finely diced
1 tbsp honey
1 tbsp balsamic vinegar
100 ml olive oil

1. Preheat the oven to 160°C.
2. Rub the beetroot with a little olive oil, wrap it in tin foil and cook for about 40 minutes, until tender. Set aside to cool.
3. Meanwhile, soak the lentils for 10 minutes if possible, rinse well and cook in a saucepan, well covered with water. Add a big pinch of salt to the cooking water. Bring up to the boil and gently simmer for 10 to 20 minutes, until they're just soft. Drain and rinse under cold water to refresh. Drain again and set aside.
4. Heat the wine in a saucepan and boil until reduced by half. Take off the heat and add the onion, honey and vinegar. Slowly whisk in the olive oil.
5. Slice the skin off the beetroot, then cut into small dice. Add to the lentils and add the vinaigrette. Mix well and serve while still warm.

Beetroot and lentil vinaigrette

Celery and olive salsa

Makes enough for 4 garnishes

This is a nice simple salsa that goes really well served with pan-fried trout or salmon. I've made this recipe using fairly average olives and it was fine, but if you have some gourmet ones you've just brought home from your own private olive grove in Tuscany, go for it – and consider me for adoption. If your raisins have been sitting in your cupboard since 1982, put them in a bowl with some boiling water to plump them up, then drain and proceed as below.

100 g raisins
3 tbsp capers
50 ml olive oil
a good splash of white wine vinegar
1 big head celery, chopped

approx. 200 g green olives, pitted
  and chopped
a handful of chopped parsley
loads of freshly ground black pepper

1. Mix the raisins, capers, olive oil and vinegar together and leave to marinate for 10 minutes or 1 hour if you have time to spare. Mix with the remaining ingredients and season well. This will last for a few hours in the fridge.

Roast aubergine with curry yoghurt

Roast aubergine with curry yoghurt

Serves 4 to 6 as a side dish

This aubergine dish is a great side order that will inevitably take centre stage and would be yum served with grilled lamb. The curry yoghurt would also be lovely served with boiled new season potatoes. Don't believe the nonsense that salting aubergines will remove all the bitter juices. If the aubergines are bitter to begin with, they'll be bitter at the finish. End of story.

for the roast aubergines:
2 aubergines
50 ml olive oil
salt and freshly ground black pepper

for the curry yoghurt:
1 x 250 g tub Greek yoghurt
2 cloves garlic, crushed
2 tsp turmeric
2 tsp curry powder
juice of 1 lemon
a good pinch of caster sugar
salt and freshly ground black pepper
a big handful of basil leaves, to garnish
a small handful of toasted pine nuts,
    to garnish

1.   Preheat the oven to 220°C.
2.   Slice the aubergines into 2 or 3 cm-thick slices. Lay out on a plate or baking tray and sprinkle generously with salt. Leave for 10 to 15 minutes and wipe off the water and salt from the aubergines with kitchen paper. Lay out on a clean baking tray, daub each slice with olive oil and season again with some salt and pepper. Roast in the oven for about 30 minutes, until golden brown. If you want, flip them over halfway through cooking. (When they're done, you can serve them warm with the yoghurt drizzled on top, or else refrigerate them for up to 3 days and serve cold with the yoghurt.)
2.   To make the curry yoghurt, mix the yoghurt with everything except the basil and pine nuts. You can add 1 tablespoon water if it's too thick. Season.
3.   Lay the aubergines out on a platter and drizzle the curry yoghurt on top. Garnish with some basil and toasted pine nuts.

Roasted red peppers with halloumi, olives and bitter greens

Serves 4 to 6

I'm partial to this for lunch or dinner and love serving it up on a big platter or straight from the roasting tin with more olive oil glugged on top, which you should dunk some tasty bread into. The colours rock and the flavours shine!

4 red peppers
olive oil
sherry vinegar
salt and freshly ground black pepper
2 onions, finely chopped
1 x 250 g pack halloumi, diced
50 g Russian cabbage or curly kale, very finely chopped
50 g pitted black olives

1. Preheat the oven to 180°C.
2. Cut the red peppers in half and scoop out the seeds. Place the peppers on a baking tray skin side down and drizzle generously with olive oil and sherry vinegar. Season with salt and pepper and cook for 15 minutes.
3. Meanwhile, heat another splash of olive oil in a frying pan. Sweat the onion for a few minutes, then add the halloumi and cook for another 5 minutes, until it starts to turn golden brown. Add the cabbage or kale and cook until it's wilted and tender. Add the olives, then taste and check the seasoning. The olives and halloumi make it pretty salty, so you probably just need pepper.
4. Fill the peppers with the mix and cook for 15 minutes in the oven. (Or you could allow them to cool fully and cook them later.) Serve warm.

*This dish demands
sunshine and a
glass of rosé.*

sted red peppers

Baked sweet potatoes
with lemon and chilli

Baked sweet potatoes with lemon and chilli

Serves 4 to 6

3 sweet potatoes
olive oil
peel and juice of 1 lemon
2 red chillies, halved and deseeded
100 ml olive oil
2 tbsp chopped coriander
a pinch of sugar
salt and freshly ground black pepper

1. Preheat the oven to 200°C.
2. Wash the spuds and leave the skin on. Chop them in half, then into quarters or eighths, depending on their size – you want chunky wedges. Drizzle with some olive oil and cook for about 30 minutes, until tender and starting to brown.
3. Meanwhile, make the sauce. Remove the skin of the lemon, trying not to get too much bitter white flesh. You really do need as much lemon as possible, so take your time and use a small, sharp knife. Whizz all the remaining ingredients together in a food processor and check the seasoning. Drizzle onto the warm potatoes and serve.

This is a nice way to jazz up some sweet potatoes if you're stuck for ideas.

Caramelised endives

Serves 6

I love sourdough bread and when left with the tail ends of a stale loaf, I sometimes stash them in my freezer for emergency toast. I get slagged off for doing this, as inevitably the lumps of stale frozen bread end up in the bin. But now I've found the ideal recipe that will justify the stale frozen bread mountain.

50 g butter
2 tbsp honey
6 Belgian endives, cut in half lengthways
salt and freshly ground black pepper
50 g sourdough breadcrumbs
70 g Parmesan
2 tbsp fresh thyme leaves
olive oil

1.   Preheat the oven to 200°C. Line a baking tray with parchment paper.
2.   Heat half the butter and 1 tablespoon honey in a large non-stick frying pan until foaming. Fry 3 of the endives flat side down until they start to caramelise. Season well. Once they've turned slightly golden brown, carefully turn them over so they get coated in the butter. Lay them out on the lined baking tray, with the good-looking caramelised side facing upwards. Wipe out the pan with some kitchen paper, then heat the remaining butter and honey and repeat with the remaining endives.
3.   Mix the breadcrumbs with the Parmesan, thyme and black pepper. Bind with a bit of olive oil. Gently pack the breadcrumbs onto the endives and bake for about 25 minutes.

Avocado, tomato and spring onion salsa

Serves 8 as a garnish

This is delicious served with loads of carrot sticks if you want to be good, or on char-grilled toast for a tasty snack.

6 cloves garlic, peeled
2 tomatoes
2 red chillies
1 whole lemon, skin and most of the white pith cut off
a big pinch of salt
a big pinch of sugar
4 ripe avocados
2 bunches spring onions, finely chopped

1. Put everything except the avocadoes and spring onions in a food processor and whizz until smooth. (I don't remove the seeds from the chillies for this recipe.) Add the avocadoes and process until smooth. Taste and add more of anything to get the desired heat or garlic kick. Mix in the spring onions and serve.

Purple sprouting broccoli with lemon and hazelnuts

Serves 2 as a side dish

A lovely, simple dish.

50 g butter
1 tbsp hazelnuts, chopped
zest and juice of 1 lemon
salt and freshly ground black pepper
250 g purple sprouting broccoli

1. Melt the butter over a low heat. Add the hazelnuts and turn up the heat. When they're just starting to brown, add the lemon zest and juice and season well. Beware of splashes of hot fat. Set aside and keep warm.
2. Trim any stalky bits off the broccoli. Blanch in boiling water for 1 minute, then drain and serve immediately with the hazelnut butter spooned over.

Artichoke, broad bean, pea and lemon salad

Serves 4 to 6

Use frozen veg for this salad, which I've tweaked from the Ottolenghi cookbook, but if you have to use tinned artichokes, drain and rinse them like crazy.

125 ml white wine
60 ml olive oil
1 tbsp pink peppercorns
2 cloves garlic, sliced
2 bay leaves
a few sprigs of thyme
50 g butter
100 ml water
250 g artichokes
250 g peas
250 g broad beans
1 lemon, thinly sliced
1 small bunch parsley, chopped

1. Heat the wine, olive oil, peppercorns, garlic, bay leaves and thyme together in a saucepan for 10 minutes, so that the wine reduces and mellows in flavour.
2. In a large saucepan, heat the butter and water until just simmering. Add the vegetables, lemon and parsley, tossing the veg for a minute or two, until they're only just cooked. Strain and toss with the warm peppercorn vinaigrette. Serve warm.

Roast Parmesan parsnips

Serves 6 as a side dish or nibble

These look as though they're fried, but in fact they're baked. They're pretty hassle free to make, even though they look as though they require dunking, dipping and frying. Well worth every delicious bite! This is adapted from a recipe in Sarah Raven's gorgeous *Garden Cook-book*.

olive oil
4 or 5 big parsnips
salt and freshly ground black pepper
50 g flour
100 g grated Parmesan
100 g breadcrumbs
2 eggs, beaten

1. Preheat the oven to 190°C. Oil a baking sheet and put it in the oven to heat up.
2. Peel the parsnips and cut into wedges. You should end up with about 550 g to 600 g of prepped parsnips after peeling and trimming them. Cook the wedges in boiling water for 5 minutes, then drain and put them back in the saucepan with a tea towel over them to help them dry out. You can leave them on a very low flame, but keep an eye on them. You just want them to dry out as much as possible. Season them well with plenty of salt and pepper.
3. Season the flour well and pour it onto a plate. Mix the Parmesan with the breadcrumbs and put them on a second plate. Have your beaten eggs ready in a shallow bowl. When the parsnips are cool enough to handle, dip them into the flour, then egg, then Parmesan crumbs. Do this quickly and put them onto a clean plate. When they're all done, put them onto the hot baking sheet and roast for about 35 minutes, until golden brown all over. You may want to turn them over halfway during cooking. Season well and serve. They're good with chilli jam or garlicky mayonnaise.

Roast
Parmesan
parsnips

Pesto potatoes

Serves 4 to 6

I adore these, even though I'm not a big fan of jars of pesto. I think most kids love pesto pasta, but I find the commercial stuff oily and tasteless. Freshly made pesto is a real treat, but because so many shoddy restaurants and cafés seem to drizzle everything with pesto, it's become as unfashionable and reviled as the poor old sun-dried tomato. Still, jarred pesto works just fine in this recipe, which is one of the tastiest ways to eat baked spuds. Don't eat them when piping hot, as you don't get the full whack of flavour that you get when they've cooled down a little.

6 good-sized potatoes
200 ml crème fraîche
200 g grated white cheddar
2 cloves garlic, crushed
2 tbsp pesto
salt and freshly ground black pepper
100 g grated Parmesan

1. Preheat the oven to 200°C.
2. Wash the spuds and score them so that you can open them up easily after they're baked. Place them straight into the oven and bake them for 45 minutes to 1 hour. Don't use any foil or oil – you're just looking for crispy skins and soft flesh inside.
3. Mix the crème fraîche with the cheddar, garlic and pesto. Set aside.
4. When the spuds are cooked, cut them fully in half and either let them cool down a little or else hold onto them with a tea towel and scoop out the flesh into the crème fraîche mixture. Place all the empty skins on a large baking tray. Lightly mash the potato and crème fraîche mixture well, season and taste. They should be über-tasty. Generously stuff the cheesy mixture back into the spuds. You may be left with a little cheesy spud mixture that just won't fit, but I tend to overstuff them. Top with the grated Parmesan. At this stage you can leave them to cool down, even overnight.
5. When ready for their final blast, cook them at 200°C for 25 to 30 minutes, until golden brown and bubbling over. Let them cool down for at least 10 minutes before serving.

Crushed spuds with watercress and horseradish

Serves 4 to 6 as a side

I had some watercress, fresh horseradish and a load of Greek yoghurt in the fridge, so naturally it all got smashed together with mashed potatoes and wolfed down while still warm. Initially I reckoned it would be fantastic served with some rare beef, but it's also perfect on its own, as long as you have a hearty appetite, a big spoon and some reverence for the humble spud. Mind you, a poached egg would be damn tasty on top.

Regarding quantities, I used one 250 g tub of Greek yoghurt and the spuds were a bit dry, so that's why I added the extra bit of crème fraîche. You basically want about 300 g of Greek yoghurt/crème fraîche to get the right consistency.

1 kg new or small potatoes
30 g fresh horseradish, finely grated
1 x 250 g tub Greek yoghurt
a few tbsp crème fraîche (if you have it)
50 g watercress, roughly torn
salt and freshly ground black pepper

1. Cook the spuds in plenty of boiling salted water, until just tender. Drain the spuds and dump them in a large bowl, then do a really poor job at mashing them so that they're just crushed.
2. Mix together the horseradish, yoghurt and crème fraîche. Add to the spuds along with the watercress and season well. Serve warm.

Crushed spuds with watercress and horseradish

Asparagus with citrus and Tabasco butter

Serves 8

This makes a large amount of butter, but it's worth doing a big batch and then freezing any leftovers in some cling film, which you could roll into a sausage shape and slice as you need it.

200 g butter, softened
1 heaped tbsp Dijon mustard
1 tbsp Tabasco sauce
zest of 1 lemon
zest of 1 orange
a pinch of sea salt
coarse black pepper
allow 6 to 8 asparagus spears per person

1. Mix the butter in a bowl with the rest of the ingredients, apart from the asparagus, and chill until required.
2. Cook the asparagus (or any veg – broccoli works great too) in loads of boiling water until just cooked, then toss immediately with a good knob of the citrus butter and eat. Alternatively, rinse the veg in cold water until you want to serve it, then heat a big knob of the citrus butter in a saucepan and quickly sauté the veg until hot and serve. Chuck an extra knob of butter on top and call the cardiologist another time.

Asparagus with citrus and Tabasco butter

Roast chickpea and aubergine salad

Serves 4

2 x 400 g tins chickpeas, drained
50 ml olive oil
salt and freshly ground black pepper
1 aubergine, diced
1 tsp soy sauce
1 tsp hoi-sin sauce
1 tsp sweet chilli sauce
1 small bunch coriander, finely chopped
a squeeze of lemon juice
1 clove garlic, crushed
1 bag of baby spinach

1. Preheat the grill to its highest setting.
2. Place the drained chickpeas on a roasting tray and pour over half the olive oil. Season with salt and pepper and grill for about 20 minutes on a high shelf – do keep an eye on them. You want them to be slightly crunchy on the outside but still fairly soft in the middle.
3. Meanwhile, heat the remaining olive oil in a large frying pan and fry the aubergine over a high heat until it starts to brown. The aubergine will absorb the oil very quickly, but only add a drop more oil if you really have to, i.e. if they're super dry and just not browning (otherwise they'll just end up saturated with oil). Turn up the heat again and add the soy, hoi-sin and sweet chilli sauces and the coriander. Cook for a further 5 minutes. Check the seasoning and add a squeeze of lemon juice, the garlic and spinach.
4. Mix the chickpea and aubergine mixture together well and serve.

This dish is a handy way to make a bag of spinach into a full-blown supper.

Ceps with potatoes and garlic

Serves 2

This could be a side order to my Death Row dinner of fillet steak and Caesar salad. It just doesn't work as a dish for six – it's best done in small batches.

200 g waxy spuds, such as Charlottes
3 tbsp olive oil
200 g ceps
50 g butter
4 cloves garlic, thinly sliced
salt and freshly ground black pepper
a squeeze of lemon juice
1 bunch flat-leaf parsley, roughly chopped

1. Cook the unpeeled spuds in boiling water until tender. Drain. When cool enough to handle, slice them into 1 cm-thick rounds.
2. Heat the olive oil and fry the ceps for 3 to 5 minutes, until they're just starting to colour. Add the butter, garlic and sliced spuds and season well. Mix carefully so the spuds don't break up. If you can be a bit cheffy, this is where tossing them in the pan, minus implements, works out quite well.
3. Add a squeeze of lemon juice and the parsley and toss them around again. Throw in another knob of butter if you're feeling skinny and serve.

Ceps with

potatoes and garlic

Show-off 5

I think we all try to show off just a little when we have friends or family over for dinner. It's hugely satisfying (for me, anyway) to feed people until they're happy and full, with contented bellies, offering up the odd 'thanks' for what they've just eaten. But when the pressure is on and there are guests coming over who you don't know that well, then the last thing you want to do is make a dog's dinner of, er, dinner. This is why I rely on the dishes in this chapter, as they provide a little wow but with a seat-belt on, because white-knuckle-ride cooking for strangers is far too stressful.

The smell of roasting meat is pretty amazing and always gets taste buds going, so buy yourself time with a few fancy nuts or olives if starters are too much hassle. And don't feel obligated to serve three courses – one good course should be plenty! Bear in mind too that you can cheat your way out of cooking all night by serving some nice dark chocolate or even a bit of cheese if dinner has been on the light side. Endlessly running to and from the kitchen is never fun. It's great to have the hard work over when you've dished up the main course and not have to fret about whether or not the next course is burning in the oven.

And practise! The reason chefs are such good cooks is that they cook every darned day and are confident that they can fix things if they go wrong. So find a dish you like and cook it often so that you get to know it intimately, hopefully tweaking it to suit your own tastes. If you have a few – or even one – of these under your belt, you'll find that they become second nature so that you can always churn them out no matter how tricky your guests might be.

113

Roast spiced loin of lamb

Serves 4

This marinade can also be used for roast leg of lamb. This cut of meat is very expensive, but definitely worth it for a special occasion. In this recipe, I've used 500 g to feed 4 people, which may seem a little stingy, but if the loin has been well trimmed, there will be very little waste. If you're worried about not being able to satisfy big appetites, then serve this with the gratin potatoes on p. 115.

500 g loin of lamb

for the marinade:
2 cloves garlic, crushed
50 ml olive oil
50 ml balsamic vinegar
1 tbsp honey
1 tsp cumin seed
1 tsp fennel seed
1 tsp mustard seed
a few sprigs of thyme
salt and freshly ground black pepper

1. Preheat the oven to 200°C.
2. Put all the ingredients for the marinade except the salt together in a large bowl or gratin dish and mix well. Add the lamb, cover and marinate overnight if possible, but 1 hour will do.
3. Before cooking the lamb, take it out of the fridge and leave at room temperature for about 15 minutes. Heat a large frying pan until very hot. Season the lamb generously while still in the marinade, then carefully place the loin in the pan. Quickly sear on all sides until well browned. Pour in the remaining marinade, transfer back to the gratin dish and cook in the oven for a further 8 minutes.
4. After removing the lamb from the oven, allow the meat to rest by covering it with foil and leaving it for at least 5 minutes before slicing and serving. Do let the meat rest or else it will look well done and dried out. Resting gives the juices a chance to redistribute evenly.

Gratin potatoes

Serves 4 to 6

I never fail to get loads of compliments for this version of pommes dauphinois. The secret is simple: I cook the potato and cream mixture in a large saucepan for about 10 minutes before transferring it to a gratin dish. This really helps to ensure accurate seasoning, as you can taste the seasoned mixture before it goes in the oven, as opposed to endlessly layering up spuds, cream, salt and pepper but not really knowing what it tastes like.

Traditionally, pommes dauphinois is made by rubbing a gratin dish with some butter and a clove of garlic, followed by layers of spuds, cream, salt and perhaps a little nutmeg. I prefer to do mine with less cream (milk instead) and loads more garlic. If serving with lamb, I wouldn't top this with cheese, but if you're serving this as a main dish for a veggie midweek supper, then by all means top it with cheese, which should go all brown and crispy.

a knob of butter
1 kg all-purpose large potatoes, washed and thinly sliced (leave the skins on)
300 ml cream
300 ml milk
2 or 3 cloves garlic, crushed
salt and freshly ground black pepper
200 g grated cheese (Swiss or mozzarella are good) (optional)

1.	Preheat the oven to 180°C.
2.	Rub the gratin dish with butter. Put the sliced potatoes, cream, milk, garlic and some salt and pepper in a large saucepan and gently bring to the boil. There should be enough liquid to just cover the potatoes. If not, top up by adding equal quantities of milk and cream, or even a splash of water. Cook the potatoes by gently simmering the mixture for 5 to 10 minutes, but don't abandon this mixture, as the cream and milk burn very easily if you don't stir it occasionally or have it on too high a heat in the first place. Taste the cream mixture to make sure it's salty enough. Remove from the heat, scoop out the spuds and layer them fairly neatly in a gratin dish. Pour the creamy liquid on top, making sure there's enough to just cover the spuds.
3.	Top with grated cheese and bake for 35 to 40 minutes. Stick a knife into the centre to check that the potatoes are very soft – you shouldn't feel anything remotely crunchy! If you do, cook for another 15 to 20 minutes. Remove from the oven and let the gratin sit for about 5 minutes before serving.

Caesar salad dressing

Makes enough for 8 salads

Don't get me started on Caesar salads in restaurants. Suffice it to say that most chefs think it's simply beneath them to make and many restaurant critics, fed up with its ubiquitous presence, see it as a sad barometer of a restaurant's inability to produce anything really original. 'Tis a pity, because a well-made Caesar salad is fantastic. (See p. 118 for a recipe for croutons.)

Tips:
- No one will want to kiss you after eating this.
- The egg yolks must be at room temperature or they won't thicken.
- Add the oil very slowly at the start. Once it has started to thicken, you can speed up the oil flow. Make it with a whisk (and get whisk elbow) or in a blender or food processor.
- If it curdles or splits, stop mixing. Start off with a fresh egg yolk and add the curdled mixture back to it very slowly.

4 egg yolks, at room temperature   1 tbsp white wine vinegar
1 tbsp Dijon mustard   1 tbsp Worcestershire sauce
300 ml sunflower oil   1 tsp fine sea salt
100 ml olive oil   a pinch of caster sugar
6 cloves garlic, crushed   freshly ground black pepper
zest and juice of 1 lemon   100 g finely grated Parmesan (optional)

1. Whisk the egg yolks with the Dijon mustard and add less than 1 teaspoon of sunflower oil. Keep whisking and add a few drops more. Add a few more and you should feel it start to change consistency. Literally add droplets at a time until you can feel a definite change in texture. Once it has started to thicken, you can start pouring the oil in a very light stream. Add about 200 ml of the oils and then add all the remaining ingredients except the Parmesan. It will get slightly watery again with the addition of liquid.

2. Resume whisking in the remaining oil, again slowly at first, and then pour it in a steady stream. Decide on a consistency you like. Sometimes if it's too thick, I add a few tablespoons of water. Taste it. Add the Parmesan if you like. Leave the flavours to develop for an hour or so, then taste it again. This will keep in the refrigerator for up to 1 week, provided your eggs were pretty fresh.

Croutons

Makes enough for 4 portions

These are evil, especially when drowned in Caesar salad dressing. Add these croutons to 2 heads of washed Cos lettuce, a handful of Parmesan shavings and a few spoonfuls of dressing for a great Caesar salad.

3 or 4 slices (about 300 g) good white bread, like sourdough
3 tbsp olive oil
50 g butter
3 cloves garlic, crushed
salt and freshly ground black pepper

1. Preheat the oven to 140°C.
2. Cut the bread into bite-sized pieces. Let them go stale by leaving them out for an hour, but if you don't have time, don't worry.
3. Heat the oil and butter in a non-stick pan until the butter is foaming, then add in the bread. Stir and try to evenly coat the bread with the oil and butter. Let the croutons turn golden brown and keep moving them about, otherwise they'll burn quickly. Once they have started to colour, remove from the heat, add in the garlic and season well. Mix it all around, then transfer onto a baking tray and bake for about 20 minutes, occasionally shaking them around in the tray, until golden brown. Allow them to cool.

Ham hock and green lentil salad

Serves 2 as a dinner or 4 as a starter

When I went to pick up the ham hocks for this recipe, the butcher told me he couldn't even give them away so didn't bother to keep them in stock. As a result, we got them for €1 each. But like plenty of cheap cuts, trends catch on and the price will go up, so grab 'em while you can. This is adapted from a Simon Hopkinson recipe.

for the salad:
1 ham hock
2 stalks celery, roughly chopped
1 carrot, roughly chopped
1 onion, roughly chopped
2 bay leaves
a few sprigs of tarragon
1 glass white wine
100 g green lentils
3 spring onions, finely chopped
2 cloves garlic, peeled and crushed
1 bunch parsley, chopped
200 g lettuce, mache or mixed leaves

for the dressing:
1 tbsp Dijon mustard
2 tsp English mustard
1 tsp caster sugar
150 ml olive oil
2 tbsp tarragon vinegar
a few sprigs of tarragon, chopped
salt and freshly ground black pepper

1. Put the ham hock in a big saucepan, cover with water and bring up to the boil, then drain. Add the celery, carrot, onion, bay leaves, tarragon sprigs and wine to the pan. Place the ham hock on top, cover with water, bring up to the boil and simmer with a lid on for at least 2 hours. Leave to cool in the liquid.
2. Rinse the lentils under cold water, then put in a saucepan with a few ladles of the ham hock liquid, enough to cover the lentils. Simmer for 15 to 20 minutes, until tender.
3. While the lentils are cooking, remove the ham hock from any remaining cooking liquid, remove the fat and discard it. You can do this by tugging away at the skin and fat and trimming with a knife. Tear off shards of meat and set aside.
4. Meanwhile, to make the dressing, mix the mustards and sugar together, then slowly whisk in the olive oil until it reaches a mayonnaise-type thickness. Add the vinegar and chopped tarragon and season well. Set aside.
5. Strain the lentils and mix with the spring onions and garlic while warm. Add the parsley and a few spoonfuls of the dressing. Add the ham hock and more dressing, pile up with some lettuce and serve.

Potato and Jerusalem artichoke soup

Serves 4 to 6

This is very rich. I used oyster mushrooms, but you can use whatever mushrooms you like. Porcini would be fabulous, but Portobellos will do. If you have it, add a few drops of truffle oil at the end.

5 large potatoes, peeled and chopped
500 g Jerusalem artichokes, peeled
3 cloves garlic, peeled
60 g butter
250 ml cream
250 ml milk
salt and freshly ground black pepper
200 g mushrooms, thinly sliced
chopped fresh parsley, to garnish
Parmesan shavings, to garnish

1. Put the spuds, artichokes and garlic in a large saucepan and fill with cold water. Bring to the boil and simmer till the spuds are practically disintegrating. Drain and put back in the saucepan with half the butter. Add the cream and milk and gently heat up.
2. I then blitzed this in a blender, and because the spuds were cooked to hell, I reckon most of the starch was long gone, hence the soup didn't go all gooey. Put the mixture back in the saucepan and heat until just simmering. Season well. (You can either serve it now or let it cool down fully and reheat before serving.) If it's too thick, add more milk or cream but make sure you season it again.
3. Fry the mushrooms on a high heat in the remaining 30 g butter and season well. Serve the soup with mushrooms on top, then garnish with some parsley, Parmesan and a few drops of good olive or truffle oil.

Olive oil poached salmon with tarragon and pink peppercorns

Serves 4

This poached salmon recipe is a real favourite and we cook a fancier version of it when catering for large buffet parties. Even though salmon is relatively fatty in comparison to something like monkfish, you would think that poaching it in olive oil would be too rich, but in fact it's bang on. It really is a great dish to do for large numbers and is grand served cold the next day or lukewarm, when it takes on an almost custard-like texture.

Don't fret if you're missing peppercorns or tarragon because you could always use green peppercorns or a few sprigs of rosemary. What's important here is the slow, gentle cooking of the fish in a salty, olive oil-based broth.

100 ml olive oil	1 small bunch tarragon
1 tbsp pink peppercorns	400 ml water
2 tsp salt	4 x 200 g salmon fillets with the skin on

1. Put the olive oil, peppercorns, salt, tarragon and water in a smallish saucepan and heat until the salt dissolves. Carefully place the salmon fillets in the saucepan – don't worry if they're all squashed together. There should be enough liquid to half-submerge them. Gently bring to the boil, then reduce the heat so that it barely simmers for about 5 minutes.

2. Turn off the heat and leave the fish in the hot liquid for about 30 minutes, turning the salmon once or twice so that it cooks evenly. You can then serve the salmon lukewarm or else cool it entirely, refrigerate it in its poaching liquid and serve cold the next day. This works really well if served with a homemade mayonnaise and some watercress salad.

Note: If you want to serve this for a large group as part of a big buffet for 30 guests, then use salmon fillets or cutlets that weigh about 120 g each and place them in a deep baking tray or casserole dish. Treble the amount of cooking liquid in the recipe above. (If you want to be thrifty, you can reuse this cooking liquid by cooking the salmon in batches.) Put about 15 fillets in your tray or casserole dish, pour the warm olive oil broth on top, cover with tin foil and cook in a low oven (140°C) for about 30 minutes. Let them cool slightly, then remove the fillets, put your next batch in and repeat the process. I wouldn't bother cooking a whole salmon this way, as the ideal thing is to have it portioned before you cook it.

Sticky spiced ribs

Serves 6

6 pork ribs, separated

for the marinade:
2 large cloves garlic, crushed
50 ml olive oil
4 tbsp tomato ketchup
2 tbsp maple syrup or honey
2 tbsp Worcestershire sauce
2 tsp fennel seeds
2 tsp cumin seeds
2 tsp roughly chopped rosemary
1 tsp smoked paprika
1 bay leaf

1. Mix all the ingredients for the marinade together. Add the pork ribs, and marinate for at least 1 hour or overnight.

2. Preheat the oven to 180°C, then cook the ribs for about 40 minutes. Cover them with tin foil if they're getting too charred. The honey/maple syrup and sugar in the ketchup will cause them to caramelise, but you can give them a final go on a hot barbecue for that charred appeal. Otherwise, turn the oven up to 200°C and remove the foil for the final 10 minutes of cooking for a cheat's barbecue effect!

This is good party food and there's no need to pull out the barbecue!

*Sticky
spiced
ribs*

Bobotie

Serves 4

Bobotie is sort of South African shepherd's pie. This recipe is best served with a big mixed salad and some warm crusty bread. You can also chuck in mustard seeds, cumin, garam masala – pretty much anything you have that's dried and spiced.

2 tbsp sunflower or olive oil
500 g beef mince
1 onion, thinly sliced
4 cloves garlic, crushed
2 tsp curry powder
1 tsp turmeric
a pinch of ground cloves
salt and freshly ground black pepper
50 ml stock or water with few splashes of
 Worcestershire sauce
2 tbsp lemon juice or white wine vinegar

2 tbsp brown sugar
2 tbsp flaked almonds
2 tbsp raisins
2 tbsp mango chutney
1 tbsp breadcrumbs

for the topping:
2 eggs, lightly beaten
150 ml milk
bay leaves, for garnishing

1. Preheat the oven to 180°C.
2. Heat the oil in a large frying pan and brown the mince for 5 to 10 minutes. Set aside.
3. In the same frying pan, sweat the onion for a few minutes, until soft, adding more oil if necessary. Add the garlic, curry powder, turmeric and ground cloves and gently sauté for 5 minutes. Season well and add the mince back into the frying pan. Add the remaining ingredients, turn the heat up and simmer for a few minutes. Taste and adjust the seasoning before taking off the heat.
4. Spoon the mixture into a well-greased ovenproof dish or 4 large ramekins. Whisk the eggs and milk together and pour the mixture over the bobotie. Spike some bay leaves into the mixture so that they resemble shark fins sticking up through the sea! Bake for 10 to 15 minutes, until the topping is set and golden brown.

Salmon en croute with dill and pistachio pesto

Serves 4

Maisha Lenehan gave me this recipe and it's delicious, even if it seems a bit old-fashioned at first glance. The flavours are great and it would be perfect to serve at a posh Sunday lunch. The pesto makes enough for six, so you'll have some left over.

for the salmon en croute:
1 x 400 g pack puff pastry
4 x 150 g fillets salmon, skinned
salt and freshly ground black pepper
1 egg yolk
1 tsp milk
a pinch of salt

for the pistachio pesto:
100 g shelled pistachios (about
    200 g unshelled pistachios)
50 g grated Parmesan
200 ml olive oil
juice of 1 big lemon
1 big bunch dill (60 g in total)
1 bunch flat-leaf parsley
salt and freshly ground black pepper

1. Preheat the oven to 180°C.
2. Blitz all the ingredients for the pesto in a food processor. Add a little more oil (or 1 tablespoon water) if necessary to get the right consistency, which is thick but spreadable.
3. Roll out the pastry a little bit on a floured surface and then cut into 4 rectangles. Roll out each rectangle so that it will easily encase each salmon fillet. Spread about 2 tablespoons pesto on each sheet, leaving 3 cm around the edges free of pesto.
4. Place the salmon fillet on top of the pesto and season the fillet with some salt and pepper. Wrap it up neatly and trim off any excess pastry. Combine the egg yolk with the milk and pinch of salt to make the egg wash. Turn the salmon over, brush with the egg wash and chill for 1 hour or overnight. Brush once more with egg wash, then bake for 30 minutes, or until golden brown.

Broad bean hummus

Broad bean hummus

Serves 8 as a nibble or 4 if served on toasted sourdough with a light salad for lunch

Homemade hummus is great for you, but you should be careful of certain tasty commercial varieties. They're often super-smooth and creamy in texture because they contain so much vegetable oil. Making hummus with broad beans instead of chickpeas is lovely – you get a soft-textured hummus in a gorgeous colour that's very quick to make and doesn't require soaking chickpeas overnight. I used frozen broad beans for this recipe because unless you can buy very young and extra-fresh broad beans, they can sometimes be a bit too pappy in texture. If you are lucky enough to find lovely fresh ones, 1 kg broad beans should yield approximately 500 g shelled broad beans.

500 g frozen broad beans
a few cloves of garlic, peeled
200 ml water
50 ml olive oil
a squeeze of lemon juice
a few sprigs of mint
salt and freshly ground black pepper

1. Boil some water and cook the broad beans and garlic for a couple of minutes, until the beans have just thawed or cooked. Drain and rinse under cold water.
2. Put the beans and garlic in a blender or food processor. Add half the water, the olive oil, lemon juice and mint. Whizz, adding a bit more water until the blades get going and start mushing the beans to a pulp. I always add too much water and thus end up with a slightly watery hummus, so go slowly. Adjust the seasoning and chill until ready to serve. It will last for a few days in the fridge.

127

Evil cheese puffs

Serves 4 to 6 as a canapé or starter

Pure vegetarian evil bites that are great for drinks parties. They're a slightly less hokey version of deep-fried brie with cranberry sauce, but close enough.

75 g butter
125 g flour, divided
approx. 400 ml milk
200 g aged Gruyère or cheddar, grated
1 tbsp Dijon mustard
2 egg yolks
salt and freshly ground black pepper
2 eggs, beaten
100 g breadcrumbs
200 ml sunflower oil

1. Make a béchamel by melting the butter in a saucepan, adding 75 g flour and cooking out for a couple of minutes. Add the milk gradually, whisking away. When it's super thick, add the cheese. Mix the hell out of it (which should feel like hard work if it's thick enough) and take off the heat. Let it cool slightly, then beat in the mustard and egg yolks. Season well and pour into a baking tray that you have lined with loads of cling film. Cool fully, then chill for a few hours. Once chilled, remove the slab of béchamel onto a board and cut into small rectangles.
2. Place the remaining 50 g flour in a shallow bowl and season it well. Put the beaten eggs in a second bowl and the breadcrumbs in a third. Then set up a conveyor belt and working quickly, dip the béchamel rectangles into the flour, then the eggs and then the crumbs. Place them on a tray. You can freeze them at this stage or chill for 1 hour.
3. To cook them, heat the sunflower oil in a small saucepan and cook for 1 to 2 minutes, until golden brown. They sometimes burst or ooze a bit, but who cares? They're pretty hardy. Serve with a relish or chilli jam.

Evil cheese puffs

Potted smoked salmon

Serves 4

175 g unsalted butter, divided
250 g smoked salmon, finely diced
150 ml crème fraîche
4 spring onions, finely chopped
1 bunch chives, finely chopped
1 bunch tarragon, finely chopped
2 tsp horseradish sauce
zest and juice of 1 lemon
salt and freshly ground black pepper
toast, to serve
mixed leaves, to serve

1. Heat 75 g butter in a frying pan and sauté the smoked salmon till it starts to go opaque. Add the crème fraîche, spring onions, chives, tarragon, horseradish sauce and lemon zest and juice. Mix gently so that the salmon doesn't go completely mushy, but making sure that everything is mixed well. Check the seasoning, then spoon the mixture into 4 ramekins. Allow to cool, then lightly press some cling film directly on top of the salmon mixture. Wrap the whole ramekin in cling film so that it's air tight. Refrigerate for a couple of hours.

2. Melt the remaining 100 g butter. Remove all the cling film from the ramekins and spoon the melted butter on top of the salmon. You can set a tarragon leaf or other herb into each one if you want to be fancy. Cover with cling film again (but don't let the cling film touch the butter) and chill for a few hours or overnight. Serve with toast and mixed leaves.

A classic recipe that demands some toast and a glass of rich white wine. You can also make this with fresh cooked crab meat instead of smoked salmon.

Spiced aubergines

Serves 4 to 6

The aubergines are worth doing if you're buying lots of bits and bobs for the blackened salmon on p. 134.

6 aubergines
a good few glugs of olive oil
1 onion, chopped
1 tsp Szechuan peppercorns
4 cloves garlic, sliced
1 chilli, deseeded and finely diced
a good knob of root ginger, peeled and finely sliced
100 ml rice wine vinegar
100 ml rice wine
2 tbsp soy sauce
1 tbsp caster sugar
freshly ground black pepper
a handful of fresh coriander, chopped

1. Chop up the aubergines into very small dice. Heat the olive oil in a big saucepan and fry the onion, peppercorns and aubergines over a high heat. If you have to add a splash of extra olive oil, do. If your saucepan isn't big enough, then fry them in 2 batches.
2. Add the rest of the ingredients, except for the coriander, and keep on a high heat until the mixture becomes quite dry. Check the seasoning and add more soy sauce if the aubergines have become too sweet or another pinch of sugar is they're too salty. Serve with some coriander.

Spiced aubergines

Pea, mint

Pea, mint and roast garlic soup

Serves 4 to 6

Unless I'm in the heart of gazpacho territory in Spain, the idea of cold soups sends a shiver of ickiness down my spine. I get the same feeling when I'm served a main course of fish with vegetable ice cream as a garnish.

This chilled pea soup, however, is a delight. You can make it with frozen peas, which, along with frozen broad beans and soy beans, have to be one of the world's handiest frozen foods. You can, of course, use fresh peas, but I find them rather inconsistent and sometimes downright horrible when bought in a supermarket, as they're inevitably flown in from Kenya or somewhere far, far away. Frozen peas are a really great product.

Serve this up in glasses as a posh starter or just enjoy a bowl of it, undisturbed, with some nice bread on a sunny day. You could also garnish this with a few peas and some small pieces of diced chorizo, which you can fry in a little olive oil.

2 to 3 tbsp olive oil
1 head garlic, broken into unpeeled
  cloves
a few sprigs of thyme
salt and freshly ground black pepper

a knob of butter
1 kg frozen peas
1 litre water
a handful of mint
200 ml cream or crème fraîche

1. Heat the olive oil in a small saucepan. Poach the garlic cloves, thyme and a little salt and pepper, covered, for 5 to 10 minutes on a very gentle heat, until just soft. Cooking the garlic this way makes it utterly addictive, but be sure to keep the heat very gentle and to cover the saucepan with a lid, because if the garlic burns, it will taste rotten. Allow to cool fully.
2. Heat the butter in a large saucepan, add the frozen peas and chuck in the water. Cook until the peas have just thawed. Squeeze the garlic flesh from their skins into the peas and add the mint. Blitz with a hand-held immersion blender or else do it in batches in your blender or food processor until smooth.
3. Pour into a bowl, add cream to taste and season well. Chill until ready to serve. It lasted a few days in my fridge and didn't lose its gorgeous Shrek-like green colour, but it will taste better if eaten within 24 hours.

Blackened salmon

Serves 4

The famous blackened cod signature dish that Nobu Matsuhisa pioneered in the Nobu restaurants is pretty tasty, but the problem with trying to recreate such magic, even with the help of his cookbook, is that his recipe relies on buying loads of Nobu's sauces and marinades, which are only available in New York. For someone dying to recreate these flavours, I spent a while trying to come up with the trademark flavour of sweet and savoury succulence.

My counterfeit version below isn't a bad fake. It's a good party dish but it does produce quite a lot of smoke, and I think it works better with salmon, which is a bit hardier when grilling in this way. It can burn like crazy on a barbecue, so the best way to cook it is on a wire rack with a baking tray lined with foil under it under a piping hot grill.

The marinade would probably be sufficient for even more salmon if you wanted to serve six or eight people.

100 ml Chinese rice wine

100 ml mirin

150 g caster sugar

a generous knob of butter

2 tbsp miso paste

4 x 200 g salmon fillets, skin removed

spiced aubergines (p. 131), to serve

1. Heat the Chinese wine and mirin in a small saucepan until boiling. Boil for a few minutes, then remove from the heat and slowly add in the caster sugar. It may bubble up when you do this, so add the sugar carefully. Whisk gently and add in the butter and miso paste. Allow to cool fully, then pour it over the fish and leave to marinate for 10 minutes or overnight.

2. Preheat the grill. When it's piping hot, quickly grill the heck out of the salmon for anything up to 5 minutes on each side (depending on how hot your grill is), as they will burn if you leave them unturned for too long. Baste them with sauce and handle them carefully, as the glaze becomes super-hot – no wandering off and answering the phone. They will only take a maximum of 10 minutes to cook. When they're all caramelised and singed on each side, serve straight away with the spiced aubergines.

Blackened salmon

Sticky

Sticky sesame chicken

Serves 4 to 6

You can make this with drumsticks or chicken breasts, but it's best to remove the skin.
Be warned: it's devilishly tasty. Allow one large or two small thighs per person.

1 tbsp sunflower or olive oil
8 skinless chicken thigh fillets
3 cloves garlic, sliced
freshly ground black pepper
50 g butter
3 tbsp soy sauce
3 tbsp fish sauce
1 tbsp sesame oil
100 g brown sugar
a small handful of sesame seeds
boiled rice, to serve
chopped spring onions, to serve
fresh chopped coriander, to serve

1. Preheat the oven to 200°C.
2. Heat the oil in a large frying pan and brown the chicken really well on all sides. Chuck in the garlic just before you transfer the chook to a casserole or ovenproof dish. Season with loads of black pepper.
3. Heat the butter in a small non-stick saucepan and add the soy sauce, fish sauce, sesame oil, brown sugar and sesame seeds. Whisk well and pour the sauce over the chicken. It may seem like you don't have much sauce, but it will get quite runny when it cooks. Bake for about 30 minutes, until golden brown and sticky. You can turn the chicken pieces over halfway through cooking and baste with the sauce. To make them really sticky and charred, grill them under a piping hot grill for a few minutes before serving. Serve with rice and loads of chopped spring onions and coriander.

Beef Wellingtons

Serves 4

4 tbsp olive oil
50 g butter
4 x 200 g fillet steaks
salt and freshly ground black pepper
a pinch of caster sugar
1 onion, very finely chopped
4 cloves garlic, crushed
250 g button mushrooms, very finely diced
a few sprigs of thyme
a splash of cream
8 to 12 slices Parma ham
1 pack ready-made puff pastry
2 egg yolks, lightly beaten

1. Heat half the olive oil and half the butter in a large frying pan till very hot. Sprinkle the top of the steaks with salt, pepper and a little sugar and brown the meat, seasoned side down, for a few minutes. Sprinkle some more seasoning onto the other surface, then turn them over and sear the other side for a few minutes, till you get plenty of charred colour without any real cooking taking place. Once you've got some decent colour on the steaks, remove them from the pan and leave to cool while you cook the mushroom duxelle.

2. Clean out the saucepan, heat the rest of the olive oil and butter and fry the onion till soft. Add the garlic, mushrooms and thyme and cook on a high heat, as you want to cook the heck out of the mushrooms so that you end up with a very dry mixture. Add the cream, season and cook until the mixture is über-tasty and dry. Set aside to cool.

This is much easier to master than you thin,
and I don't bother making the pancake b
either – too much stodge and hassle

3. When the steaks and mushrooms are cool, lay out 3 sheets of cling film (to give extra strength to your parcels) on top of each other. Lay out 3 to 4 slices of Parma ham and spread them lightly with a layer of mushrooms. Place a steak in the centre and wrap up in the ham, then pull up all sides of the cling film to meet at the top. Twist the cling film around so you end up with very tight bundles. Repeat with the remaining steaks and chill for a few hours.

4. We're trying to keep the pastry from rising, so roll it into a ball, then roll it out quite thinly and divide it into 4 sheets. Unwrap the beef from the cling film and wrap it in the pastry, using a little beaten egg to seal the top. Cut away any excess pastry and use your fingers dipped in water to smooth out the seams and ensure the pastry is snug against the beef. Place the ugly sealed side down onto a plate that you've lined with some parchment paper. Brush the tops with egg yolk and chill until ready to bake.

5. Heat the oven to 190°C and preheat a non-stick baking sheet. Just before baking, lightly score the pastry with a sharp knife, but don't cut all the way through. Cook the beef, straight from the fridge, until the pastry is golden brown and the beef is medium rare, which should take 12 to 15 minutes. If you want them more well done, turn down the oven to 160°C so that the pastry doesn't burn and bake for an extra 5 to 10 minutes.

Buffalo mozzarella, black olive and grape salad

Serves 4 as a starter

This recipe has to be credited to two fab lady chefs, Alice Waters from Chez Panisse in California, via *Sally Clarke's Book* from her London restaurant, Clarke's. It's a firm favourite for dinner parties and will be sure to win you silly amounts of praise. Follow the advice about good ingredients here, as skimping on them for this recipe will elicit soggy applause rather than rock-star cheers.

150 g good-quality black olives
1 clove garlic, crushed
1 small red chilli, deseeded and finely sliced
1 tsp capers
30 ml olive oil
1 tbsp balsamic vinegar
coarse black pepper
3 balls buffalo mozzarella, drained
1 small red onion, very finely sliced
350 g seedless black grapes, halved
chopped fresh parsley and coriander
good-quality bread, to serve

1. Mix the olives, capers, vinegar, garlic, chilli and olive oil together. Season with pepper and marinate for 30 minutes.
2. When ready to serve, slice and arrange the buffalo mozzarella onto individual plates. Add the onion and grapes to the olive and caper mixture, mix well and spoon onto the plates. Drizzle with extra olive oil and some herbs. Serve with some good bread.

Buffalo mozzarella, olive and grape salad

Steeped chicken with spring onion and ginger sauce

Serves 4

I adapted this dish from a Ken Hom recipe. Reading through some of his recipes, it's clear that preparation and good techniques are very important in Chinese cooking. Steeping is one such method, often used for fish or chicken, and is different to poaching in that you immerse your chicken or fish in stock or water before bringing it to the boil. Then you gently poach it for a while before turning off the heat and letting it gently finish cooking. The result is a beautifully tender texture that's almost satiny.

for the steeped chicken:
1 chicken
1 tbsp sea salt
1 bunch spring onions
a few slices of fresh ginger
freshly ground black pepper

for the spring onion and ginger sauce:
100 ml olive oil
3 large bunches spring onions, finely chopped
3 cloves garlic, peeled and finely chopped
a big knob of ginger, peeled and finely chopped
2 tbsp soy sauce
1 tsp sesame oil (optional)

1. Put the chicken in a large saucepan that you can fit a lid onto and cover with water. Chuck in the rest of the ingredients and cook on a gentle heat until just simmering. Keep the lid on and simmer for 15 to 20 minutes, then take off the heat and keep covered with the lid for 1 hour.

2. Meanwhile, to make the spring onion and ginger sauce, heat the olive oil in a saucepan until hot but not smoking. Place the spring onions, garlic and ginger in a bowl. Pour the hot oil over the spring onion mixture and mix well. The heat of the oil will cook the spring onions, garlic and ginger just enough. Add the soy sauce and sesame oil and adjust the seasoning to your taste.

3. When the chicken is fully cooked, remove it from the saucepan, but be careful of hot water pouring out of the bird! Check it's cooked by slicing between the breast and the leg to make sure it's not pink, but if it is, place it back in the water, bring back up to a simmer and leave the chicken in the water for another 10 minutes. Remove the skin and discard. Tear off the chicken in chunks and place it onto a platter with a bowl of the spring onion and ginger sauce.

Ridiculously tasty prawns

Serves 4

I recently snatched a packet of raw prawns on some sort of dodgy supermarket offer and shoved them in the freezer for a 'bad mommy' day. That's a day when there's nothing left in the house to eat except a bit of old bread in the freezer, a few cloves of garlic and a tin of baked beans. It's also when I'm prone to shrieking at 8 p.m., 'Not to worry, dinner will be ready in a jiffy!'

The family sat around the table, confirming they weren't eating porridge at night or any 'baked beans and prawns' combo. For a moment, I thought I may have been on to a thrifty version of surf 'n' turf, but luckily common sense prevailed. This dish ended up as a kind of gourmet prawns on toast that was truly delicious and repaired my damaged reputation somewhat. Feel free to add loads of chopped flat-leaf parsley. If you serve this with plenty of bread and a salad, you may just get away with allowing 100 g prawns per person.

50 ml olive oil
8 cloves garlic, unpeeled
a few sprigs of thyme (if you have it)
salt and freshly ground black pepper
a knob of butter

400 g raw prawns (or whatever you can get!)
a splash of white wine
crusty bread, to serve
green salad, to serve

1. Heat the olive oil in a small saucepan and cook the whole, unpeeled garlic cloves very gently for about 3 or 4 minutes. Cover with a lid to stop any oil from splattering. Add the thyme and season lightly. If the oil gets too hot, the garlic will burn and become bitter. If that happens, start again with new cloves of garlic.

2. Stick a knife into one of the cloves and if it's soft, remove the cloves from the oil and drain on kitchen paper. Leave them until they are cool enough to handle.

3. Heat the knob of butter and an extra splash of olive oil (left over from the garlic confit) in a large saucepan. Fry the prawns on a high heat until they start to get a good colour and caramelise in parts. Squeeze the garlic from its skins and add to the prawns along with the wine and plenty of black pepper. Squish the garlic with a wooden spoon and mix well, sautéing the prawns until cooked through (which should only take a couple of minutes). Serve with loads of bread and a green salad.

Pork and lettuce parcels

Serves 4 to 6 as a starter

The pork balls are a little bit bold because they do contain some sugar and salty fish sauce, but I like them because they're tasty and you don't have to fry them. Cut down on the sugar and you'll have quite a lean, mean fighting machine of a dish.

for the pork balls:
500 g minced pork
1 red onion, finely chopped
3 cloves garlic, crushed
2 stalks lemongrass, very finely
 chopped
2 tbsp caster sugar
2 tsp cornflour
50 ml fish sauce
1 bunch mint, finely chopped
1 bunch coriander, finely chopped

for the lettuce parcels:
2 or 3 Baby Gems
1 cucumber, peeled and grated
1 red onion, finely sliced
juice of 1 lime
a splash of sweet chilli sauce
chopped fresh mint and coriander

1. Preheat the oven to 200°C.
2. Mix all the ingredients for the pork balls together. Roll the pork mixture into little balls and place on an oiled baking tray and cook for 15 to 20 minutes. You may want to shake them around during cooking, as they tend to burn and stick because of the sugar. Feel free to bake them on a baking tray lined with lightly oiled parchment paper.
3. Meanwhile, to make the little salad boats to serve them in, wash and separate a few heads of Baby Gem lettuce. Mix the cucumber and red onion together, then add the lime juice, a splash of sweet chilli sauce and some extra chopped coriander and mint. Place a pork ball in each lettuce leaf and top with the cucumber and red onion mixture.

Cider poached turkey with maple chilli glaze

Serves at least 10

This idea came from Paula McIntyre's recipe for brining turkey, which I did one year for my *Irish Times* column. When we went to photograph it, I was way behind schedule so I ended up boiling the heck out of the turkey to hurry it along so we could take a photograph of it! The result was so good, and when I thought about it, the steeping method works for the steeped chicken on p. 142, so why not try it for the turkey?

1 x 3–4 kg turkey crown
100 g butter, softened
salt and freshly ground black pepper

for the poaching liquor:
50 g sea salt
50 g Demerara sugar
2 litres cider
2 litres water
2 cinnamon sticks
1 onion, chopped
zest and juice of 2 oranges
a handful of fresh sage, rosemary and
  thyme, chopped

for the maple chilli glaze:
1 small red chilli, deseeded
1 onion, finely chopped
a big knob of ginger, peeled
1 tbsp olive oil
200 ml cider
4 tbsp maple syrup
2 tbsp cider vinegar
salt

1. You can prep the maple glaze by sweating the chilli, onion and ginger in the olive oil for a few minutes. Add the rest of the ingredients and gently simmer until reduced by half. Strain and discard the bits of ginger and onion, etc., then continue to cook gently until reduced to a syrupy consistency. Set aside.

2. To poach the turkey, place it in a large pot with all the poaching liquor ingredients. Bring up to the boil and simmer for 20 minutes, then turn off the heat and leave to steep in the hot liquid for 2 hours. You can allow it to cool fully in this liquid.

Cider poached turkey with maple chilli glaze

3. When you're ready to serve, preheat the oven to 190°C. If you can, shove your hand under the turkey skin and spread the butter across the bird so that it forms an extra layer between the skin and turkey breast. If not, just dot the butter on top. Season well and roast, covered with tin foil, for 45 minutes, or until golden brown and hot. If you have a meat thermometer, it should read at least 74°C. Baste the turkey with the maple glaze every 15 minutes or so. If you can do it more often than that, happy days. Let the turkey rest for at least 20 minutes before carving.

Smoked trout with parsle
and capers on w

Smoked trout with parsley and capers on walnut and raisin toast

Makes enough for 4 to 6 sandwiches

This is also perfect as a good brunch dish, especially on toasted pumpernickel bagels. It makes enough for approximately 20 generous canapés or four to six open sandwiches. Everything except the toasts can be done well in advance or the night before and refrigerated.

6 slices raisin and walnut bread
200 g cream cheese
200 g smoked trout
freshly ground black pepper
2 tbsp capers
2 tbsp olive oil
1 tbsp Dijon mustard
zest and juice of 1 lemon
1 bunch of parsley, finely chopped
1 bunch of spring onions, finely chopped

1. Toast the bread and set aside. Mix the cream cheese and trout together using a fork to mash the trout and season well with black pepper. In a separate bowl, mix the capers with the remaining ingredients.
2. Top the toasts with the cream cheese and trout mix, spoon some of the caper mix on top and serve.

Chicken parcels with green chilli sauce

Serves 4 to 6 as a nibble

These are a favourite, the only downside being that they need to be cooked and eaten pretty quickly. They're perfect for more relaxed, fun entertaining – think beer and paper towels. Make a massive batch and don't bother cooking anything else for dinner!

for the green chilli sauce:
2 green chillies, deseeded
2 spring onions
2 cloves garlic
1 avocado
juice of 3 limes
1 tbsp olive oil
a splash of sweet chilli sauce
a handful of fresh coriander
salt and freshly ground black pepper

for the pastry:
175 g plain flour
25 g butter
90 ml warm water

for the filling:
1 tbsp olive oil
1 onion, very finely chopped
1 large skinless chicken breast
200 ml tomato juice
6 cloves garlic, crushed
2 tbsp raisins
a handful of green or black olives,
   very finely chopped
½ tsp cumin
a pinch of dried chilli flakes
a pinch of cinnamon
a pinch of ground cloves
salt and freshly ground black pepper
1 litre sunflower oil, for frying

Chicken parce

1. Make the chilli sauce by whizzzing everything in a blender or food processor. Check the seasoning and refrigerate until ready to serve.

2. Make the pastry by whizzzing the flour and butter in a food processor until it resembles crumbs. Add the warm water, which will turn it into a soft dough. It's a fairly sturdy, tough pastry, so roll it out on a floured surface until quite thin, but still hardy enough to take the chicken stuffing and not tear apart when folded. Cut into 7.5-cm rounds, which is about the width of a water glass. When they're all cut, chill for 1 hour while you get the chicken mix ready and cooled down.

3. Heat the olive oil and sweat the onion until soft. Chop the chicken into chunks and mince in your food processor until it's mush. Add the tomato juice and garlic to the frying pan and gradually add the minced chicken. Break up the chicken with the side of a wooden spoon, as it will want to stay in one big lump. Once it has started to move around, add the rest of the ingredients except the sunflower oil. Cook on a high heat until most of the liquid has evaporated and the mixture is quite dry. Check the seasoning to make sure it's good and tasty. Allow to cool fully before stuffing the pastry.

4. Place a spoonful of filling on one half of a pastry disc and fold the other half over, making a half-moon shape. Use a little water in a cup beside you to dampen the edges of the pastry, which will help make the edges stick together, before pressing them closed. At this stage, you can keep them for 48 hours in the fridge in single layers.

5. When you're just about ready to serve, heat a few inches of sunflower oil in a medium-sized saucepan and fry the parcels until golden brown and crisp. Drain on kitchen paper and season with a sprinkle of salt. Serve with the green chilli sauce.

Roast shoulder of lamb

Serves 4 to 6

This is good enough to eat as a main dish, but when it cools down, use shards of this for the lamb salad on p. 153. Both recipes are lovely, but I have Geoff Lenehan to thank for the roast shoulder recipe. It's truly delicious. You could eat this for two on night one, then make the salad and serve another four the next day.

1.6 kg lamb shoulder on the bone
2 heads garlic
a few sprigs of rosemary
olive oil
salt and freshly ground black pepper

1. Preheat the oven to 220°C.
2. Line a roasting tin with a large enough sheet of tin foil that you'll be able to wrap the lamb up in it, then place the lamb in the tin. Cut the garlic heads horizontally and plonk into the roasting tin along with some rosemary, a good drizzle of olive oil and seasoning.
3. Wrap up in the tin foil and cook for 30 minutes on a high heat. Turn down the oven to 170°C and cook for another 3½ to 4 hours. Allow to rest before carving and serve slices of lamb with your favourite spud dish. Keep leftovers for the salad on p. 153.

Roast shoulder of lamb

Roast lamb salad

Serves 2

for the lamb:
leftover roast lamb (p. 152)
a few splashes of soy sauce
a sprinkle of sesame seeds

for the dressing:
3 tbsp mayo
3 tbsp vinegar
1 tbsp soy sauce
1 tbsp English mustard
1 tbsp smooth peanut butter
1 tbsp sweet chilli sauce
1 tsp sugar
1 tsp tahini
2 cloves garlic, crushed
1 green chilli
juice of 2 limes
salt and freshly ground black pepper

for the salad:
2 or 3 Baby Gems
1 cucumber, sliced
1 red onion, sliced
1 bunch mache (lamb's lettuce)
1 bunch spring onions, chopped
1 bunch coriander, roughly chopped
1 bunch mint, roughly chopped

1. Whizz all the ingredients together for the dressing. Add some hot water if it's too thick. Check the seasoning and adjust as necessary.
2. Heat up your grill. Place shards of lamb on a baking tray. Sprinkle with some soy sauce and sesame seeds. It's usually fatty enough that you shouldn't need any olive oil, but if it looks a bit dry, give it a splash with some. Grill for 5 to 10 minutes, until it's starting to char.
3. Mix the salad ingredients together, toss with some dressing and top with hot grilled lamb. Serve straight away.

Roast lamb salad

Tasty barbecued lamb

Tasty barbecued lamb

Serves 8 to 10

This works best with leg of lamb; shoulder is just too darned grizzly and fatty. If I'm going to put it on the barbecue, then I make sure to use a boned leg of lamb, but if I have to cook it in the oven, then I'll leave the bone in, marinate it and roast in the oven at 200°C for the first 20 minutes or so, then reduce the heat, cover with foil and cook for 18 minutes per ½ kg at 180°C. Thanks to Oisin Clarke for this recipe.

1 boned leg of lamb
4 cloves garlic, crushed
250 ml red wine
200 ml soy sauce
1 big bunch mint, roughly chopped
approx. 25 g rosemary sprigs
freshly ground black pepper
quinoa and pomegranate salad (p. 158), to serve

1. Put the lamb in a big dish that will fit in the fridge. Mix the rest of the ingredients together and pour it over the lamb. Leave to marinate overnight, if possible, occasionally turning the lamb over so that the marinade penetrates evenly.

2. Heat the barbecue and cook the lamb for about 20 minutes on each side, basting regularly with the marinade. The cooking time completely depends on the thickness of the meat, so you need to keep an eye on it after about 30 minutes or so. If you feel it's getting too charred but want to keep it cooking if it still feels a little too fleshy and raw, then wrap the lamb in tin foil. This will stop the naked flame from attacking it. Allow to rest for at least 10 minutes before slicing and carving thinly.

157

Quinoa and pomegranate salad

Serves 2 to 3 (allow 70 g per person)

I first came across quinoa on a yoga week-of-hell holiday with my sister. At every meal time, the yoga instructors served mounds of gloopy quinoa salad, waxing lyrical about all its benefits. I kept thinking they should fertilise fields or make tyres out of it instead of inflicting it on humans. Consequently, I haven't been able to face it since then, and even the pronunciation of it (keen-wah) used to make me queasy. That was until the super-gorgeous nutritionist Susan Jane Murray served a fantastic curried quinoa salad for dinner one night and converted me to its magic.

You cook quinoa in two parts boiling water to one part quinoa. Once the water has boiled off, cover with a lid and let it steam for another 5 minutes or so. The grains will look like they have burst open ever so slightly and it will still have some crunch when you taste it. Drain and eat hot or let it cool down fully and use as you would if making a light pasta salad, potato salad or couscous-type salad. Don't use mayonnaise, but rather olive oils, vinaigrettes, fresh squeezes of lemon, lime or orange juice, lots of herbs, seasoning and that's about it.

You can buy both the Marigold stock powder and quinoa in health food stores or good food shops. This is good served with the barbecued lamb (p. 157).

250 g quinoa

1 tbsp curry powder

2 tsp turmeric

1 heaped tsp Marigold stock powder

50 g raisins

3 cloves garlic, crushed

zest of 1 lemon

a good glug of olive oil

2 pomegranates or 100 g
   pomegranate seeds

2 tbsp pine nuts

1 bunch coriander, roughly chopped

1. Cook the quinoa in twice as much water as quinoa. Add the curry powder, turmeric and Marigold. Simmer for 10 minutes, until most of the water has evaporated. Add the raisins and take off the heat. Partially cover with a lid and let it steam for another 5 to 10 minutes.

2. Stir in the crushed garlic and lemon zest. When cooled down slightly, add the rest of the ingredients. Serve warm or cold as a salad.

Quinoa and
pomegranate salad

*Crab cakes with lemon
and caper salsa*

Crab cakes with lemon and caper salsa

Serves 4 to 6

for the crab cakes:
450 g crabmeat (cooked)
50 g Carr's Water Biscuits
1 egg, beaten
2 tbsp mayonnaise
2 tsp Dijon mustard
zest and juice of 1 lemon
a splash of Worcestershire sauce
a good few splashes of Tabasco
1 bunch flat-leaf parsley, chopped
sunflower oil

lemon wedges, to serve
mixed leaves, to serve

for the lemon and caper salsa:
100 ml olive oil
2 tsp honey
juice of 1 lemon
4 tbsp baby capers
2 bunches spring onions, finely
  chopped
freshly ground black pepper

1. Chuck the crabmeat into a large stainless steel or glass bowl and pick through it, ensuring there are no bits of shell in it.
2. Crush the crackers in a cup using one end of a rolling pin or crush them in a plastic bag or food processor. Add all the ingredients except the sunflower oil and mix really well. Don't worry if the texture feels a bit wet, they'll be OK.
3. Roll the crabmeat into balls the size of golf balls; if you happen to squeeze out a bit of juice, that's fine. Line them up on a plate or baking tray and then refrigerate for at least 1 hour. I cover them loosely, as I wanted the fridge to dry them out slightly.
4. Meanwhile, to make the salsa, simply mix everything together and set aside.
5. When you're ready to cook the crab cakes, preheat the oven to 170°C. Heat some sunflower oil in a non-stick frying pan. Line a plate or tray with kitchen paper. Fry a few cakes at a time, using a fork and spoon to gently turn them over when they're golden brown on one side. Let them colour before you try to turn them over, and do this gently, as they'll fall apart if you manhandle them. When you have a good colour on them, transfer them to the kitchen paper-lined plate to drain. You may have to change the oil if it starts getting too many bits of burned crumb in it.
6. When they're all done, you can put them on a clean baking tray and heat them up in a moderate oven (160°C) for 10 to 15 minutes while you get ready to plate up.

Nectarine, mozzarella and Parma ham salad

Serves 4

This is a nice easy starter or perfect summer lunch. This is one of those recipes that demands top-notch ingredients as it's so darned simple.

2 balls buffalo mozzarella
olive oil
salt and freshly ground black pepper
1 sprig of fresh thyme
1 clove garlic, peeled
1 x 250 g punnet cherry tomatoes
4 nectarines or peaches
juice of 2 lemons
1 big bunch basil
mixed leaves
8 to 12 slices Parma ham

1. Drain and slice the buffalo mozzarella and lay it out flat in a bowl. Drizzle generously with some olive oil and season well. Add the thyme and garlic and marinate overnight or preferably at room temperature for 15 minutes to 1 hour. You can turn the slices over so they get doused with olive oil and move the garlic around the place.
2. Slice the cherry tomatoes in half and cut the nectarines into eighths. In a bowl, gently mix the cherry tomatoes and fruit slices with some lemon juice, salt and pepper. Drizzle generously with the olive oil from the mozzarella.
3. On a big platter or 4 individual plates, lay out basil leaves and mixed leaves. Plop the Parma ham around the plates and add the nectarines and tomatoes. Add the mozzarella slices on top. Serve at once.

Nectarine, mozzarella
and Parma ham salad

Salt 'n' peppa chook

Salt 'n' peppa chook

Serves 4 to 6

This is dead easy and tasty. I used one whole chicken that was cut into six to eight pieces and fed five really greedy people. You could ask your butcher to do this for you or just buy a selection of legs, thighs and breasts (for the wussy guests). If you want to make this for eight to 10 people, then double the spices and just get as many chicken pieces as you need.

6 cloves

4 star anise

1 cinnamon stick

3 tsp Szechuan peppercorns

1 tsp fennel seeds

2 or 3 tbsp olive oil

zest of 2 limes

1 heaped tsp sea salt

freshly ground black pepper

a few sprigs of thyme

6 to 8 pieces of chicken

1. Put all the spices in a small frying pan and gently heat them for 1 minute to dry roast them. Either grind them in your grinder or pestle and mortar, or pour them into a cup and crush them with the end of a rolling pin. Off the heat, add the crushed, dry-roasted spices back into the saucepan and add the olive oil. Add the rest of the ingredients except the chicken and mix well. The residual heat from the saucepan will gently warm the olive oil and other ingredients, which will make it easier to pour and rub onto the chicken.
2. Put the chicken in a roasting tray and pour on the oily spice mixture. Rub the meat well (wash your hands well afterwards), cover with cling film and marinate in the fridge for 1 hour or overnight, if possible.
3. When you're ready to cook, you can either cook this in the oven at 190°C for about 25 to 30 minutes (less if you're just using breast meat) or cook for 15 minutes in the oven and finish off on a barbecue. It tastes great either way.

Figs with goat's cheese and Parma ham

Serves 4 as a very big starter or lunch

Unfortunately, these are a bit too ugly to photograph, which is why we've used an arty shot of figs instead, but they're absolutely delicious and deserve to be made.

8 figs
160 g semi-hard strong goat's cheese
12 to 16 slices Parma ham

olive oil
freshly ground black pepper
fresh thyme leaves
salad, to serve

1. Preheat the oven to 190°C.
2. Cut the figs nearly in half – don't chop all the way through so that they remain attached at the base. Cut the goat's cheese into 8 slices and slip one slice into each fig. Wrap the figs and cheese with the Parma ham and place on a baking tray. Drizzle with some olive oil and season with black pepper and fresh thyme if you like. Bake for about 15 minutes, until the Parma ham is crisp and has a good colour. Serve with a simple salad.

Figs

Cauliflower and blue cheese soup with pear and bacon

Serves 4 to 6

Crozier Blue or Cashel Blue cheeses go really well with this soup.

for the cauliflower and blue cheese soup:

2 onions, sliced
2 cloves garlic, chopped
fresh thyme leaves
a good knob of butter
1 cauliflower
2 bay leaves
1.5 litres vegetable or chicken stock
250 g blue cheese
100 ml crème fraîche
salt and freshly ground black pepper

for the pear and bacon garnish:

a knob of butter
1 tsp brown sugar
2 pears, peeled and finely chopped
4 streaky rashers, finely diced
1 tbsp raisins
a splash of red wine vinegar
freshly ground black pepper

crusty bread, to serve
fresh chopped parsley, to garnish

1. To make the soup, sweat the onions, garlic and thyme in the butter in a saucepan with a lid, until soft. Break the cauliflower into florets. Add to the saucepan along with the bay leaves and stock. Cook, covered, for 20 minutes or so, until the cauliflower is soft. Remove from the heat and add the blue cheese and crème fraîche. Whizz with a hand-held blender or in a food processor, then put it back in the saucepan and check the seasoning. (At this stage, you can allow it to cool down fully, refrigerate it and reheat it the next day.)

2. To make the garnish, simply heat the butter and sugar in a non-stick frying pan and fry the pears and bacon until golden brown and caramelised. Add the raisins and deglaze the pan with some red wine vinegar. Keep cooking until it turns quite sticky and season with lots of black pepper.

3. Serve the soup in big bowls with crusty bread, the pear and bacon garnish in the centre and a good sprinkling of parsley.

Korean salmon

Serves 2

This is quick, tasty and immensely satisfying to eat with a cold beer in hand. You'll have enough marinade to do a third 200 g fillet, but if you want to serve more fish, just double the marinade quantities.

2 x 400 g salmon fillets, skin removed
4 cloves garlic, finely chopped
50 ml soy sauce
4 tbsp light sesame oil
2 tbsp sweet chilli sauce
1 tbsp black or white sesame seeds
a good pinch of chilli flakes
freshly ground black pepper
chopped spring onions, to serve
salad, to serve

1. Cut the salmon into big chunks, or you can leave it whole. Mix all the other ingredients together and marinate the fish for a few hours or overnight.

2. Cook on a wire rack with a baking tray lined with foil under it under a hot grill for 5 to 10 minutes, until charred and cooked through. You can baste with extra marinade while cooking. Serve with some chopped spring onions and a salad.

Korean salmon

Sweet Stuff

6

I don't have that much of a sweet tooth, but every time I say that, my husband laughs out loud and just points to the stash of dark chocolate in the house. 'That's medicinal,' I say, because many experts say that the odd square of dark chocolate is good for you, providing endorphins and antioxidants galore.

If you have room, then a tasty, simple dessert can be a lovely treat. I couldn't be bothered with anything too intricate regarding desserts, and in many restaurants, I find the fancy desserts on offer too fiddly to be enjoyed. I like sweet stuff to be really simple and straight up. In other words, no faffing about.

Rich flourless chocolate cake

Serves 6 to 8

A simple, straightforward chocolate cake that tastes much better if left for a day.

240 g butter
270 g dark chocolate
6 eggs, separated
250 g sugar
120 g ground almonds
1 or 2 extra bars of milk or dark chocolate, broken into small squares
   (optional)
ice cream, to serve

Rich flourless chocolate cake

1. Preheat the oven to 180°C. Butter and flour a springform cake tin. (You do this by rubbing the tin with some butter, adding 1 tablespoon flour and moving the cake tin around in such a way as to evenly coat the butter with flour. Do it over a sink and tip out the excess flour.)

2. Melt the butter and chocolate in a glass bowl placed over a saucepan of simmering (not boiling) water. Make sure the bottom of the bowl isn't touching the water. You want to melt the chocolate slowly and gently.

3. Whisk together the egg yolks and sugar until good and thick. Add the melted chocolate and mix well. Fold in the ground almonds using a big metal spoon.

4. Beat the egg whites until they're frothy and forming soft peaks. Fold them into the cake mixture, and if you feel like being extra chocolaty, add the squares of extra chocolate.

5. Pour the batter into the prepared cake tin and bake for about 40 minutes, or until the sides of the cake are set but the middle is still soft and glossy. Allow to cool fully before removing from the tin and serving with ice cream.

Rhubarb fool with rosemary and ginger

Serves 4 to 6

Don't get all cranky and think I'm sticking the rosemary in here to be a bit wacky and creative in the most aggravating sense. It's really quite tasty.

500 g chopped rhubarb
1 sprig of rosemary
a knob of ginger, peeled and chopped in half
approx. 150 g caster sugar
200 ml cream

1. In a medium-sized saucepan with a lid, cook the rhubarb with the rosemary, ginger and just enough water to stop it from burning on a low heat for about 20 minutes, or until it's tender. Allow it to cool a little, then remove the ginger and rosemary. When it's still warm, add enough sugar to sweeten it. Allow to cool fully.
2. Whip the cream until thick and fold it into the rhubarb. Add more sugar if necessary. If you want to show off and have a layer of pretty pink juice on top of your fool, then simply leave the rhubarb in a sieve to cool and collect the juice, which you can then pour on top.

Light vanilla panna cotta

Serves 4

This is ridiculously simple to make. For some reason I'm always reluctant to dig out gelatine sachets, probably because they're hidden away in the Loch Ness depths of my kitchen cupboards.

You can use vanilla yoghurt instead of plain yoghurt, but if you do, you don't need either the vanilla pod or the honey, as vanilla yoghurt is sweet enough.

This recipe makes enough to fill four small espresso-sized cups or ramekins. If you're feeding six, then double the recipe.

2 tbsp honey
2 tbsp boiling water
1 vanilla pod
2 tsp gelatine (or 1 x 10 g sachet)
500 g plain yoghurt (low-fat works grand)
a few fresh berries, crushed pistachios or any kind of nuts, to decorate

1. In a jug or small glass bowl, mix the honey with the boiling water. Stand the jug or bowl in or over a saucepan of boiling water that has been taken off the heat. Split the vanilla pod and scrape the seeds into the honey water.
2. Remove the jug/bowl from the hot water, sprinkle the sachet of gelatine on top and stir until the gelatine dissolves. If it feels like it's going a bit lumpy and not quite liquid, then put the jug/bowl back in the boiling water so that the mixture can heat up again. This will help the gelatine to dissolve.
3. Once the mixture is smooth enough, add the yoghurt. Taste and add more sugar if needed. Sieve the yoghurt mixture so that it's extra smooth and any lumps of gelatine can be discarded. Spoon the mixture into 4 moulds or ramekins and chill for 3 hours or overnight. Decorate with berries and nuts.

Raspberry ice cream

Serves 4

On my long list of pet hates and things that make me *really angry* are ice cream recipes that finish up by telling you to 'freeze according to your ice cream machine manufacturer's instructions'. Bugger off, I say, because A) I don't own a home ice cream machine and B) even if I did, it would inevitably never get used because the blade would be missing.

125 g fresh raspberries
250 ml Greek yoghurt
250 ml cream, lightly whipped
100 g icing sugar
1 tsp vanilla essence

1. Put the raspberries in a large bowl and mush with a potato masher. Add in the rest of the ingredients, taste and add more sugar if needed and pour into a plastic container. After a couple of hours in the freezer, mix with the potato masher and refreeze it. Serve within 12 hours of making it, otherwise it turns too icy after that and will make you start hankering after the commercial smoothness of brand-name ice creams.

This recipe worked fabulously well using an old battered plastic container, a potato masher and a little elbow grease.

Raspberry ice cream

Mini molten chocolo

cakes

Mini molten chocolate cakes

Serves 4 to 6

These adorable little cakes of gooey chocolate are a cinch to make. Make then in small ramekins and they'll come away from the sides, which means you can turn them out as well as serving them straight from the dish. You could cook them in advance for 8 to 10 minutes and reheat if necessary, or just have them ready to go in the ramekins and bake to order.

200 g dark chocolate
100 g butter
3 eggs, beaten
120 g caster sugar
30 g flour
cream or ice cream, to serve

1. Preheat the oven to 200°C.
2. Break the chocolate into pieces. Melt the chocolate and butter in a bowl sitting on top of a saucepan of simmering water. Don't have the water level too high in the saucepan – ideally the water shouldn't be able to touch the bottom of the bowl.
3. When the chocolate and butter have melted, stir well and set aside for 1 minute. Whisk the eggs, sugar and flour together until well combined, then add in the melted chocolate mixture.
4. Place ovenproof ramekins or dariole moulds on a baking tray so that you can transport them easily. Pour the mixture into the moulds and bake for about 15 minutes, or until the edges are set. Remove and allow to cool slightly before serving with a big blob of cream or ice cream.

Note: If you want to be super decadent, then buy an extra bar of chocolate and when you've poured the chocolate mixture into the ramekins, dunk a square or two of chocolate in the middle of each pot before you put them into the oven, which will make them extra gooey and chocolaty.

Lemon semifreddo

Serves 6 to 8

This turned into a pretty decent dessert, but after initial tasting and testing it was abandoned in my freezer. During a soccer semi-final TV dinner, I pulled it out of the freezer, convinced it would have been destroyed by freezer burn. I served it up with a few raspberries to some crazed soccer fans and they reckoned it was very do-able after copious amounts of beer and curry.

6 egg yolks
150 g caster sugar
150 ml lemon juice (about 3 lemons)
zest of 1 lemon
375 ml cream, lightly whipped

You'll need a loaf tin if you want to serve this in slices, otherwise just use a plastic container.

1. Put the egg yolks, sugar, lemon juice and zest in a medium-sized glass bowl placed over a saucepan of boiling water. Whisk away, and as the mixture heats up, it will swell in volume. When it roughly doubles in volume and is light and fluffy, remove from the heat and allow to cool, giving it the odd whisk. When it has cooled fully, fold in the whipped cream.
2. Line the loaf tin with cling film, with a generous amount of cling film hanging over the edges. This is so you can lift it out like one big loaf and slice it later. Pour the mixture into the tin and freeze until solid, which should take a few hours. When you're ready to serve, use the cling film to lift it out of the tin, then slice as you would a loaf of bread.

Apricot and almond cake

Serves 6 to 8

Lovely with a cup of tea.

225 g butter
225 g caster sugar
zest and juice of 1 lemon
80 g ground almonds
3 eggs

100 g flour
150 g dried apricots, roughly chopped
honey mascarpone cream (p. 183), to serve
poached apricots (p. 183), to serve

1. Preheat the oven to 180°C. Lightly butter a standard 20–25 cm non-stick springform cake tin. You can line it with parchment paper if you want, but if it's non-stick, you really don't need to.

2. Beat the butter and sugar together in an electric mixer or food processor until light and fluffy. (You can do this by hand with a spatula or wooden spoon and lots of elbow grease.) Add the lemon zest, juice, ground almonds and eggs. Beat until well mixed and don't worry if it looks like it's going to curdle. Fold in the flour and apricots. Mix well and pour into the cake tin.

3. Put the tin on a baking tray and cook for about 40 minutes, until the cake feels firm and a skewer comes out clean. Allow to cool. Serve cold with a big blob of honey mascarpone cream and some poached apricots.

Poached apricots

Serves 6 to 8

This is delicious as a garnish to the very more-ish apricot and almond cake (p. 181), but is equally good on top of Greek yoghurt or even your morning porridge.

600 ml water
200 g dried apricots
1 cinnamon stick
seeds from 1 vanilla pod
zest and juice of 1 orange

1 tbsp honey
1 tbsp brown sugar
1 tsp freshly ground black pepper
½ tsp allspice

1. Put all the ingredients into a saucepan, heat gently and simmer for 10 minutes. Allow to cool slightly, then remove the apricots and simmer again to reduce the sugar syrup by a third. Add the apricots back to the syrup and allow to cool fully.

Honey mascarpone cream

Makes approx. 200 ml

The perfect accompaniment to cakes.

150 ml cream
3 tbsp mascarpone
1 tbsp honey
a splash of vanilla extract

1. Whisk the cream until frothy. Add the mascarpone, honey and vanilla and whisk until thick and creamy. Chill and serve as required.

Serves 4

The word 'pudding' has always put me off. I think heavy, stodgy and something only for the depths of winter. But these are always a great success and very easy to make. They will stick like hell unless you line the dariole moulds with parchment paper. To do this, cut a square of parchment paper, then crush it into a tiny ball and dampen it slightly with some water. It will be very pliable and will line the mould or ramekin much more easily. This has been adapted from a Skye Gyngell recipe.

Ginger and blackberry pudding

approx. 4 tbsp golden syrup
approx. 16 blackberries (1 small punnet)
100 g butter, softened
100 g caster sugar
2 large eggs
zest of 2 lemons
4 knobs of preserved stem ginger, finely chopped
100 g self-raising flour
a pinch of salt
whipped cream, to serve

1. Preheat the oven to 180°C. Line the dariole moulds with parchment paper (see across).
2. Squeeze or spoon about 1 tablespoon golden syrup into each mould. Drop 3 or 4 blackberries into each one and set aside.
3. Using an electric beater or the back of a wooden spoon, cream the butter and sugar in a medium-sized bowl until light and fluffy. Add the eggs, lemon zest and ginger. Mix well and don't panic if it starts to curdle. Fold in the flour, add the pinch of salt and it'll sort itself out. Spoon the mix evenly into the moulds.
4. Place the moulds on a baking tray and bake for about 30 minutes, until a skewer comes out clean. If your oven has a harsh, dry heat (like mine does and like a lot of Agas do), then cover the puddings with some buttered tin foil. Allow them to cool before removing from the moulds, then turn them upside down so that you get to see the blackberries. Serve with some whipped cream and a little leftover syrup from the stemmed ginger if you like.

Chocolate sorbet

Serves 6

Just thinking about chocolate sorbets full of icy shards of bitter darkness makes me clench my teeth in a Sensodyne sensitive teeth kind of way: it just doesn't seem right. However, we all agreed this was a mighty fine dessert, perfect for when you want a little something sweet but can't face an entire slice of anything. It's almost like eating a really rich, frozen, cocoa-dusted truffle. You could serve it with mandarin segments poached in 400 ml water along with 2 tablespoons caster sugar and a splash of orange blossom flower water. The only reason I did this was because I have two darned bottles of it in the cupboard, which I'm still trying to get rid of. This is adapted from Skye Gyngell's cookbook, *A Year in My Kitchen*.

250 g caster sugar
600 ml water
300 g dark chocolate (the higher the cocoa content, the better)
1 tbsp cocoa powder

1. Heat the sugar and water in a saucepan until the sugar has dissolved. Gently simmer for about 5 minutes. It should have some body.
2. Roughly chop the chocolate or break into small pieces and put in a bowl with the cocoa powder. Slowly pour in the sugar syrup, stirring constantly with a wooden spoon at first and then a whisk. Keep stirring or gently whisking until the mixture is smooth. Allow it to cool down until good and thick, then transfer to a plastic container and freeze for a few hours.

Chocolate sorbet

Banoffee pie

Serves 6 to 8

This is a very quick version that doesn't even require pastry, but rather crushed biscuits, like a cheesecake. Use any combo of biscuits.

1 x 410 g tin sweetened condensed milk, preboiled (see below)
300 g ginger nuts, digestives or Hob Nobs, crushed
350 g butter, divided
150 g + 1 tbsp soft brown sugar
3 bananas, sliced
250 ml cream, whipped until stiff
grated chocolate, to decorate (optional)

You will also need a 25 cm tart tin with a removable base.

1. Remove the label from the tin of sweetened condensed milk and place in a saucepan (with a lid!). Cover well with water and bring up to the boil. Cook for 2 hours in simmering water, covered, but please make sure that the tins always remain covered in water, otherwise they might explode. Because this is a bit time consuming, boil a few tins at a time, as they'll keep indefinitely and then you always have the basis of a handy dessert ready to go. Remove the tins from the water and cool for at least 4 hours before opening the tin.

2. Whizz the biscuits in a food processor or crush them with a rolling pin or saucepan in a Ziploc plastic bag that you have sealed once all the air has been pressed out. Pour the crushed biscuits into a bowl.

3. Melt 150 g of the butter, then add to the crushed biscuits. Mix well and press evenly into the tart base or individual ramekins or pots. Heat another 150 g butter and 150 g soft brown sugar in a saucepan until the sugar has dissolved. Mix well, then add the tin of cooked sweetened condensed milk. Mix well again and bring to the boil. Reduce the heat and gently cook for a few minutes, then remove and pour onto the biscuit base. Place in the fridge to chill for a few hours.

4. Heat the remaining 50 g butter in a non-stick frying pan until foaming. Add the banana slices, sprinkle over 1 tablespoon soft brown sugar and gently fry on both sides until golden brown. Allow to cool.

5. To assemble, spread the cream on top of the toffee mixture and top with the caramelised banana slices. Top with grated chocolate, if you fancy.

Panettone bread and butter pudding

Serves 6 to 8

I always have a ton of panettone in my cupboards each Christmas because of my Italian in-laws. They arrive each year en masse, with goodies from the fantastic Cracco Peck deli in Milan. It's a fair arrangement. They're allowed to stay with us for Christmas provided they bring me plenty of goodies from Peck's. They know the rules. No goodies, no Christmas dinner.

3 large eggs
1 egg yolk
100 g caster sugar
300 ml double cream
300 ml milk
2 tsp vanilla extract
1 panettone, regular size
butter
a splash of whiskey
100 g mincemeat
1 Granny Smith apple, peeled, cored and finely chopped
icing sugar, to dust (optional)
cream or Greek yoghurt, to serve

1. Beat the eggs, egg yolk and sugar together until light and fluffy. In a saucepan, bring the cream and milk up to the boil. Add the vanilla extract, then pour the cream mix onto the eggs and whisk.
2. Slice the panettone into 2 cm slices and butter each side, then layer all of them up in a large gratin dish, adding a splash of whiskey and a few dots of mincemeat and apple. Pour the cream and egg mixture over the panettone and leave to rest for 1 hour before baking.
3. Preheat the oven to 180°C.
4. Put the gratin dish in a large roasting tin and fill the tin with boiling water. Bake for 45 minutes to 1 hour. It should puff up and still be a bit runny but not super sloppy. Allow to cool slightly and dust with icing sugar if desired before serving with cream or Greek yoghurt.

Fig tart

Fig tart

Serves 6 to 8

Ideally you should make this in a 29 cm tart tin, but you can also do this in a baking tray. Whatever suits. I absolutely love this tart.

200 g plain flour
100 g butter
175 g caster sugar
a pinch of salt
1 egg yolk
1 tsp vanilla extract
10 figs, quartered
2 tbsp granulated sugar
150 g apricot jam

1. In a food processor, make the pastry by pulsing the flour and butter until it resembles breadcrumbs. Add the sugar and salt, then pulse again. Add the egg yolk and vanilla extract and keep processing until the pastry comes together and forms a ball. If it's a bit dry and won't form a ball, add a tiny splash of cream or water. Wrap in cling film and chill for 30 minutes or overnight.
2. Preheat the oven to 180°C.
3. Roll out the pastry until it will cover the base of the tin only (not the sides). It's almost like putting focaccia into the tin rather than lining something with pastry, so you can patchwork quilt the pastry rather than trying to roll it out perfectly. Arrange the fig quarters on top, sprinkle with sugar and bake for about 45 minutes, until puffed up slightly and golden brown.
4. When the tart is cool, melt the jam with a few teaspoons of water over a gentle heat. Glaze the tart with the jam and leave to cool fully before serving.

Chocolate cheesecake brownies

These are a bit more grown up than just plain old brownies, something different and not as sickly sweet as many homemade brownies.

Chocolate cheesecake brownies

Makes 12 to 16 brownies

200 g pecans

1 x 225 g pack cream cheese

510 g caster sugar, divided

200 g + 1 tbsp plain flour, sieved

1 egg yolk

5 large eggs

200 g dark chocolate, chopped

300 g unsalted butter, softened

1. Preheat the oven to 170°C. Grease a 28 x 23 x 4 cm non-stick cake tin or roasting tin and line the bottom with parchment paper.

2. Toast the pecans for a few minutes on a baking tray in the oven, then chop them roughly.

3. Whisk the cream cheese, 60 g caster sugar, 1 tablespoon flour and the egg yolk together, then cover with cling film and set aside in the fridge to chill.

4. Mix the nuts with 200 g flour and set aside. Whisk the eggs and the remaining sugar with an electric beater until pale and thick, which should take at least 5 minutes.

5. Melt the chocolate over a bowl of barely simmering water, then add in knobs of butter. Mix well. Fold the chocolate mix into the beaten eggs and sugar, then fold in the flour and nuts. Pour the chocolate mixture into the tin.

6. Using two teaspoons, drop knobs of the cream cheese mix in rows. Once you have done that, you can pat them down so that they sink.

7. Bake for at least 40 minutes. They look a bit pale rather than a dark chocolate colour, but once a skewer is reasonably clean, remove them from the oven and allow to cool before slicing.

Passion fruit and lemon meringue pie

Serves 6 to 8

I have no idea why, but if you ask me to bake a meringue I get a bit stressed, which is ridiculous, as meringues are just so darned simple that I have no excuse. Yet I always make a dog's dinner of them. It usually starts off with a fumbling of eggs, burst yolks and shattered shells. Then I forget how many eggs I've actually put into the bowl – hopeless carry-on that could be described as plain old incompetence. However, they do make a quick and tasty dessert, especially for large gatherings, which is why I'm fond of a Simon Hopkinson recipe called Angel Pies, full of lemon curd and passion fruit.

for the meringue:
3 egg whites
sunflower oil
a pinch of salt
¼ tsp cream of tartar
125 g caster sugar, plus extra for
   sprinkling
1 tsp corn flour
2 tsp white wine vinegar

for the lemon curd:
90 g unsalted butter
rind and juice of 2 lemons
125 g sugar
2 eggs, beaten

to assemble:
300 ml cream
1 tbsp caster sugar
6 to 8 passion fruit

1. To make the meringue base, preheat the oven to 120°C. Grease a 24 cm tart tin with a removable base with a little sunflower oil.

2. Beat the egg whites with a pinch of salt and the cream of tartar until they form soft peaks. Add the sugar 1 tablespoon at a time while still beating until the whites are thick and glossy. Fold in the corn flour and vinegar.

3. Spread out the meringue in the prepared tart tin, then sprinkle with extra caster sugar and bake for 1 hour. Turn off the oven but leave the meringue in the oven for another hour. Allow it to cool in the tin.

4. To make the lemon curd, melt the butter in a bowl set over boiling water along with the lemon rind, juice and sugar. When they are well mixed, add the beaten eggs and mix well. Cook for 10 to 15 minutes over the simmering water, until thick, then allow to cool.

5. To assemble, whip the cream along with 1 tablespoon caster sugar. You can mix the whipped cream with the lemon curd or do a separate layer of cream and a separate layer of lemon curd on top of the meringue, whatever you prefer. Spoon the flesh from the passion fruit on top of the pie and serve.

Tips

- Any trace of egg yolk in the egg whites will make it impossible to stiffen the egg whites.
- Your equipment – a metal or glass bowl and whisk or beater – must be *spotlessly* clean. Any trace of fat on your equipment will make it very difficult to properly stiffen the egg whites. Plastic bowls can still be a bit greasy – even if you've cleaned them scrupulously.
- Use egg whites that are at room temperature because they will reach a greater volume. A general rule of thumb is that older eggs are better for whisking, as they're less gelatinous, which is a good quality when you're poaching eggs for breakfast, but not when you're looking for serious volume from whisking.
- Cream of tartar helps stabilise the egg whites.

Coffee ice cream

Serves 6 to 8

Where does one get muslin? In a maternity shop! You can buy a bag of 10 pieces, which are great for straining cloudy sauces or this ice cream recipe.

600 ml milk
120 g coarsely ground coffee
5 egg yolks
150 g sugar
400 ml cream
6 tbsp Tia Maria

1. Bring the milk and coffee to the boil, then remove from the heat and leave to infuse for 30 minutes.
2. Meanwhile, whisk the egg yolks and sugar until pale and thick. Put a glass bowl in the freezer.
3. Strain the milk and coffee mixture through muslin and back into a clean saucepan. Add the egg and sugar mixture and stir gently over a low heat to make a coffee custard. Don't cook the heck out of this – you want it to thicken slightly, not turn into scrambled eggs. Pour into the chilled bowl and whisk in the cream and Tia Maria. Keep stirring until it gets cold, then either freeze in a plastic container or else use an ice cream machine.

Apple tart

Serves 6 to 8

Old-fashioned goodness. This isn't great reheated or served the next day, so make it and gorge on the same day.

1 kg Bramley or other cooking apples, peeled and diced (about 5 big apples)
225 g golden caster sugar, plus extra to decorate
1 tsp ground cinnamon
juice of 1 lemon
1 tbsp corn flour
375 g frozen puff pastry, thawed
milk
cream or ice cream, to serve

1. Preheat the oven to 180°C. Grease a 24 cm tin.
2. Toss the diced apple with the sugar, cinnamon, lemon juice and corn flour.
3. Roll out two-thirds of the pastry. Line the tin with it and let the excess pastry flop out over the sides. Tip the apple mixture into the tart tin and brush the edges of the pastry with milk. Take the last third of pastry, roll it out and cover the apples, pressing the apples down and pressing the edges of the pastry together so that it seals up the tart. Trim the excess pastry, brush the surface with milk and sprinkle with extra sugar.
4. Make 6 incisions in the pastry to let the steam out. Bake for 30 minutes, then lower the heat down to 150°C and cook for another 40 minutes, until golden on top. If it's looking a little flaccid, keep cooking until it's golden. Cool slightly and serve with cream or ice cream.

Angela and Nicky's lemon cheesecake

Serves 10 to 12

Nicky is a dear old friend of my sister's and is a fabulous caterer in England. Her sister, Angela, gave us this recipe years ago, and I remember it fondly from when I was a young lass. It's beyond simple, but always goes down well.

I used a 28 cm tart tin with a removable base, but the recipe would probably squeeze into something a tad smaller.

1 x 300 g pack Hob Nobs or digestives
100 g butter, melted
2 x 225 g packs cream cheese
1 x 410 g tin sweetened condensed milk
zest and juice of 2 lemons
fresh berries, to serve

1. Whizz the biscuits in a food processor or crush them with a rolling pin or saucepan in a Ziploc plastic bag that you have sealed once all the air has been pressed out. Pour the crushed biscuits into a bowl and mix well with the melted butter. Pat the crumbs into the base of the tin and then chill for 1 hour or so.
2. Using an electric beater, mix the cream cheese, condensed milk, lemon zest and juice. Smooth onto the top of the biscuit base with a spatula, but do this carefully or you'll end up mixing up the base in with the cream cheese. Respect the layers! Chill for another few hours or overnight and serve with some berries.

Hazelnut tart

Serves 8 to 10

One of our restaurant managers, Emma Donoghue, nicknamed this a Ferrero Rocher tart, and she's right. That's exactly what it tastes of, especially if you serve it with some hot chocolate! This is adapted from a Skye Gyngell recipe.

for the pastry:
250 g plain flour
125 g unsalted butter
30 g caster sugar
2 large egg yolks
zest of 1 lemon
1 tsp vanilla extract

for the filling:
300 g skinned, roasted hazelnuts
300 g caster sugar
300 g unsalted butter
3 eggs
zest of 1 lemon

1. Whizz all the pastry ingredients together in a food processor until it forms a ball. Wrap in cling film and chill for 1 hour. Roll out the pastry between two sheets of cling film and line a 25 cm tart tin. Prick the base with a fork and chill again for 30 minutes. Preheat the oven to 180°C. Line the base with parchment paper and some rice or beans and bake for 10 minutes. carefully remove the hot beans/rice and bake for another few minutes to dry out the pastry. Set aside to cool while you make the filling.
2. To make the filling, preheat the oven to 190°C. Whizz all the filling ingredients until they're smooth but still retain some nutty texture (don't overprocess). Place the prepared tart tin on a baking tray, then pour the filling into the tart tin. Bake for 45 minutes. If it starts to turn too brown, then lower the oven temperature, but it should be a nice golden brown colour and almost have the texture of treacle tart. Allow to cool slightly and serve warm or cold.

Lime ice cream with

Lime ice cream with cajeta

Serves 4 to 6

Cajeta is a kind of Mexican caramel and this makes one tasty dessert.

for the lime ice cream:
250 ml cream
250 ml crème fraîche
150 g granulated sugar
1 tbsp tequila or rum
1 tsp vanilla extract
zest and juice of 3 limes

for the cajeta:
2 litres goat's milk
200 g granulated sugar
1 cinnamon stick
1 tbsp lukewarm water
½ tsp bicarbonate of soda
mint sprigs, to decorate

1. To make the ice cream, mix all the ingredients together and freeze in a plastic container or an ice cream machine.
2. To make the cajeta, heat the goat's milk, sugar and cinnamon stick until simmering and cook for 10 minutes. Mix the water with the bicarbonate of soda. Take the saucepan off the heat and carefully add the bicarbonate water to the goat's milk mixture (it can bubble up, so be careful). Whisk away, then put back on the heat and gently simmer for 2 to 3 hours, until it's thick and golden brown. If it starts to burn, you may have to transfer it to a non-stick saucepan and keep reducing it down. Mine eventually went a bit lumpy, so I added a few tablespoons of warm water, whisked away the lumps, put it through a sieve and continued to cook it down until I got the flavour and consistency right.
3. Drizzle the cajeta over the lime ice cream, decorate with mint sprigs and serve.

jeta

Cherry and orange pudding

Serves 6 to 8

The corn flour just helps to keep the juice syrupy and rich. The trick is to make this dessert before you wolf down too many cherries while removing the stones...

1 kg cherries (about 900 g when stoned)
50 g Demerara sugar, divided
1 tbsp corn flour
zest and juice of 1 orange
a few sprigs of thyme or rosemary, leaves finely chopped
100 g butter
125 g caster sugar
2 eggs
100 g ground almonds
vanilla ice cream, to serve

1.   Preheat the oven to 180°C. Butter a gratin dish. Mine is about 37 x 23 cm, but anything fairly shallow will do.

2.   Stone the cherries with a knife and your fingers or with a fancy stoner. Place them in a bowl with half the Demerara sugar, the corn flour, orange zest and juice and thyme. Pour into the gratin dish.

3.   Beat the butter and caster sugar until light and fluffy. Add the eggs and ground almonds and beat well.

4.   Spoon the mix in blobs onto the cherries and smooth it out with a wet spatula so that it covers most of the cherries. Sprinkle the topping with the rest of the Demerara sugar and bake for 45 minutes, or until golden brown and bubbling. Serve warm with vanilla ice cream.

Cherry and
orange pudding

Strawberry

Strawberry cake

Serves 6 to 8

This cake can seem a bit too moist in parts, so don't worry if the skewer comes out a bit crumby. The combination of simple flavours is a little old-fashioned, but it looks lovely and tastes like something a sweet grandmother would make for your birthday.

220 g flour, sieved
3 tsp baking powder, divided
180 g caster sugar
180 g butter, melted
140 ml warm milk
4 eggs, separated

2 tsp vanilla extract, divided
450 g strawberries
2 tbsp icing sugar
250 g mascarpone
250 ml cream
2 or 3 tbsp honey

1. Preheat the oven to 180°C. Grease a 22 cm springform cake tin.
2. Mix the flour with 1 teaspoon baking powder and the sugar. Add in the melted butter and milk and whisk using an electric beater. Whisk in the egg yolks and 1 teaspoon vanilla extract.
3. In a separate bowl, whisk the egg whites until soft peaks have formed. Add the remaining 2 teaspoons baking powder to the egg whites. Fold the egg whites into the flour mixture, then pour into the greased tin and bake for 45 minutes, or until a skewer comes out clean. Allow to cool fully.
4. Remove the hulls from the strawberries and sprinkle the berries with the icing sugar. Whisk the mascarpone with the cream, honey and remaining 1 teaspoon vanilla extract. Spread the mascarpone on top of the middle of the cake (which you could slice in half). Top or sandwich with the strawberries, which you could slice in half or leave whole. Serve. This cake doesn't hold well, so make, decorate and eat it on the same day.

Index